D1609395

KERAMOS

KERAMOS

FRANZ F. KRIWANEK

REVISED EDITION

THE TEACHING OF POTTERY

KENDALL/HUNT PUBLISHING COMPANY
DUBUQUE, IOWA

400279   02

67.282

"I went down to the potters house, and
there he was working at his wheel. And the
vessel he was making of clay was spoiled in
the potters hand. And he reworked it into
another vessel, as it seemed good to the
potter to do."

JEREMIAH 18:3

To Hermie

Contents

Foreword

To write this foreword is indeed a privilege hoped for, but not expected because there are a number of great potters who are Franz's friends and well-wishers. I am most pleased because as educators both he and I are philosophically committed to the crafts and are practicing craftsmen. In Keramos, he has shown that the craftsman stands at another great point in history and has the opportunity now to become a most meaningful part of an affluent, technological society which is searching for richer meanings in life.

Franz Kriwanek is not simply a teacher who makes pots, nor is he a potter who must teach to support himself. He is at one and the same time an inspired teacher, an excellent potter, and a profound humanist philosopher. The crafts are indeed fortunate to have such a spokesman for he presents the potential of the crafts as cultural and individual fulfillment in almost visionary proportions. The ideal he shares in Keramos demonstrates his rare insight into the motivation of man, the artist. The fruits of his research in clays and glazes, his studio and market experience raise the book to new heights of practicality. Craftsmen and large segments of our populace may reach a harmonious relationship of mutual benefit when the message of Keramos is "experienced." The text and the photos are consistent with the finest goals he has always set and consistently achieved for himself. It is in his studio work and his writing that pottery has become superlatively human. Franz has my greatest respect as a co-worker and contributor to the literature of pottery and therefore does a service for mankind.

Dr. Foster Marlow
San Marcos, Texas

Preface to the Second Edition

In less then three years KERAMOS has gone into a second, revised edition. The acceptance of the book by students and instructors across the country has been heart warming. During the past two years I have been carefully listening to ideas, suggestions, and a lot of advise. I have attempted to incorporate as many of these ideas in the new edition.

Many new, unpublished photographs have been added to clarify and to inspire the student. A chapter on glaze calculations and an automatic glaze calculator in form of conversion charts enrich the glaze chapter. Information regarding the construction of a simple potterswheel, and an extended appendix give even more "potters-hints" then before. Those are the new features of the second edition.

With all the new enrichment of the book, the philosophy of KERAMOS remains the same, that is; to offer as much technical information to the student as possible, within a humanistic framework. Keramos is not the kind of book a student can become addicted to, the book alone is not supposed "to do it," it allows the instructor to complement the contents with his own style of teaching and his own methods which he derived from his experiences with the material and the craft.

Again, I must thank the many artist-potters who so generously responded to my call for ideas and photos. Their full and friendly cooperation made the book possible. I hope sincerely that the new KERAMOS will be of a real value to them and their students.

Franz Kriwanek
Silverton, Colorado

Preface

The purpose of Keramos is to provide the teacher of pottery with a text which presents the necessary technical know-how of pottery making within a long overdue humanistic context. The paramount task of writing this book was to evoke in the student an awareness of the intrinsic values and characteristics of the material while he is struggling with problems of skill and practice. I have always admired the philosophy perpetrated by the Bauhaus which taught students a solid foundation of technical know-how while surrounding the learner with a highly charged, inspiring atmosphere conducive to creative activity. The need for this book became obvious to me once I recognized that the bulk of the existing literature in the field of pottery concerns itself primarily with the promulgation of technical data and processes.

Keramos has not been written for the ceramic engineer, nor for the glaze chemist. It approaches both interest areas of engineering and glaze chemistry from a creative approach, an approach which will especially serve well the artist-potter, who is basically a creative improvisor, and thinks more along the lines of art than chemistry. Nevertheless, Keramos does offer all necessary techniques for initial success. For the teacher of pottery, on beginning and intermediate levels, it will simplify his task significantly by motivating the students to outrun their own imagination. Also, the extensive appendix, with its wealth of ideas, charts, and formulas should make the book of value to both the student and the practicing potter.

My most sincere thanks must go to the many potters and teachers who touched my life, and whose influence upon my personal development has sparked the desire within me to write Keramos. My family and my close friend Foster Marlow, I thank for their unreserved help and patience during the many months this work was in process.

F.K.
San Marcos,
Texas

Figure 1.

Chapter I

New Concepts in Clay

WHAT IS CLAY?

Clay is the first step in the creation of pottery. KERAMOS is a book for potters. It is only natural, therefore, that it concerns itself first with clay. Many of the concepts that we consider "new" today have in fact been around for centuries, but no one has bothered to observe and record them into information useful for the artist-potter. The "new" in KERAMOS lies in its clues as to where and how to find clay, how to prepare it, and, it is hoped, how to use it. This is important for anyone who is seriously interested in ceramics.

Clay is pliable, alive, responsive earth which is impressionable when in a plastic state. It can be found everywhere for it is the most abundant material present on this planet. *Keramos* means *burned earth.* In actuality, clay is decomposed rock which can be made to conform to the potter's form-feeling by the use of water, and then by being subjected to extreme heat can be returned to its rocklike state.

KERAMOS is not a book for chemists or geologists, for its interest lies not in the mapping or investigation of large, commercially-valuable clay deposits. Rather, its purpose lies in a belief that love of clay is still possible in our mass-producing twentieth century society. Through an intimate concern for prospecting and preparing the material, the potter will experience a higher plane of appreciation. After all, every work of art should represent an intimate fusion of the artist's spirit with the materials he is using.

Basically, clay consists of alumina and silicates combined with a variety of impurities. A typical chemical analysis of a surface clay as it can be found almost anywhere in the United States may look like this:

Silica	49.98 percent
Alumina	17.52 percent
Volatile matter	7.88 percent
Calcia	5.50 percent
Magnesia	1.82 percent
Iron	1.00 percent
Undetermined residue	16.30 percent

It is probably unnecessary to point out that almost all clay deposits vary in their chemical composition and that the term *typical* can be applied only in a general sense. The individual differences in the chemistry of clay deposits depend on the type of clay, its location, its origin or formation in the past, and its contamination by alkalies and metals during the formative ages. The advanced artist-potter interested in clay as a medium of expression does not appreciate or evaluate clay by its chemical components. Potters are much more interested in the "feel" of clay, its color, texture, and firing range. These are defined as the physical properties of clay, and are more significant for the artist even if, in the final analysis, they depend upon the chemical components of the material.

The alumina and silica contents of a clay remain fairly constant with different deposits. It is the organic matter—roots, fossils, grasses and such, including the fractional impurities of metals and alkalies—that vary significantly from location to location. These variations are of great interest to the artist-potter as they make a particular clay uniquely typical of its location. This is one of the major factors that makes the effort to prospect for one's own local clay worthwhile. There is almost unanimous agreement among persons in the field that the use of one's own local clay is an advantage. The involvement in prospecting for the clay adds depth and meaning to the work, and inadvertently, because of the unique chemistry of the clay, assures uniqueness in texture and color which always enhance the work of an artist. As such, the clay one uses can become a loyal ally in the potter's continuous search for expression.

Clays are usually divided into two distinct types, *residual* and *sedimentary*. The artist-potter is interested in both types, as each has special functions and uses in studio work. *Kaolins* and *china clays* are of the residual type, which means that these clays have been found in the original position of the mother-rock. Residual clays are mostly mined. They must undergo a number of purifying processes before they are ready for the market. When sold, they are available in the form of fine powders (some finer than 200 mesh) and are ready for use as additives in clay-bodies and glazes. Ball clays, some fire clays, natural stoneware clays, and common red clays are *sedimentary* in origin. This means that the clay particles have been carried by erosion into streams, lakes, and lagunes where they settled to the bottom in still waters. Through ages of evolution they finally formed thick layers of fine-particled mud. On their way to their final resting place they intermixed with particles of organic matter, metals, and whatever they may have picked up on their way down. Naturally, coarse particles settled faster because of their weight, and the smaller particles

Figure 2. Basically clay is decomposed rock. A close-up of clay from a commercial quarry reflects the "rock" quality of fairly pure clay.

Figure 3. The edges of rivers and dry river beds are good sources of readily available sedimentary clay samples.

were carried further by the waters. Ball clays are very "small particled" clays and because of this they serve as very good additives where more plasticity is required in a local clay. Sedimentary clays are found in many large deposits connected with brickyards, with pipe and tile-producing plants, and with terra cotta factories. When such clay quarries are near, they are almost always useful to the artist-potter. The managers of such yards have the information on the clay and are usually helpful to the artist in aiding him to make use of their clay. After a move, it is useful to locate the nearest brickyard.

The author in his studio now uses a clay-body which has a simple composition of:

100 pounds	Fire clay
100 pounds	Ball clay
100 pounds	Brick clay

This body will stand temperatures up to cone 11, though it fires best at cone 8-9. When fired higher, it becomes somewhat brittle and chips easily. The texture of this body is enhanced by an addition of 15 percent of fine grog, part of which consists of soft, ground, red bricks. The addition of ground bricks causes large reddish-brown spots when covered by any feldspatic glaze and properly matured. In reduction, the body assumes a dark, warm, brown color which is very attractive. Another thoroughly tested body can be devised from local clays for temperatures below cone 7, best fired to cone 5-6,

300 pounds	Brick clay
100 pounds	Fire clay
100 pounds	Ball clay

This body displays a fine rust-brown color in an oxidizing atmosphere and is somewhat darker in reduction. Its only drawback is the limitation in temperature.

In cities and towns, building supply companies provide another good source of inexpensive clays. These are marketed finely ground and therefore do not have to be sun-dried before prepara-

Figure 4. The monolithic, rough clay form of stoneware clay express the primeval character of clay well. Cone 8, heavily grogged stoneware, Bengt Berglund, Gustafsberg, Sweden.

Figure 5. A tiny deposit cropping out from the surface. Clay from this deposit has been used in the cone 7 body by the author. The clay was screened through a twenty mesh screen and the natural sand content of the clay eliminated the need for grog in the body.

tion. The trade names for such clays are *Fire clay* and *Mortarmix*. Mortarmixes are highly plastic, red, common clays and are used as additives to mortars to improve their stickiness. One should always make sure that the label on the bag states that the content is pure clay. Fire clays are widely known and are used by builders to line fireplaces, furnaces, and heating plants. They should be prepared for use the same way as any raw clay except, as has been pointed out before, they do not have to be dried before use. When properly prepared, wedged, and aged, they compare favorably with purchased clay-bodies. The aging of self-prepared clays is always very important and will be dealt with later.

When funds are available, clay-bodies can be purchased pre-packaged from ceramics dealers. These clay-bodies are carefully composed and are always quite safe for their intended uses. By the same token, the careful composition eliminates much of the excitement and charm that self-processed clay can provide. The opening of a package of clay may save a few hours of time and effort, but it also diminishes the intimate understanding and contact the artist should have with his material. It is in the character of the artist-potter to search for the unique, to take a chance, to experiment and discover. While some of these clays are acceptable, they have never really been intended for the artist, but are rather planned for "mass" production. The lively effects, gradations, and changes in color and texture are automatically a part of self-prospected, natural clays because of their ample impurities and variations in chemistry.

Figure 6. A large surface clay deposit along a road cut in Delaware.

MAP OF THE CLAY DEPOSITS OF THE UNITED STATES

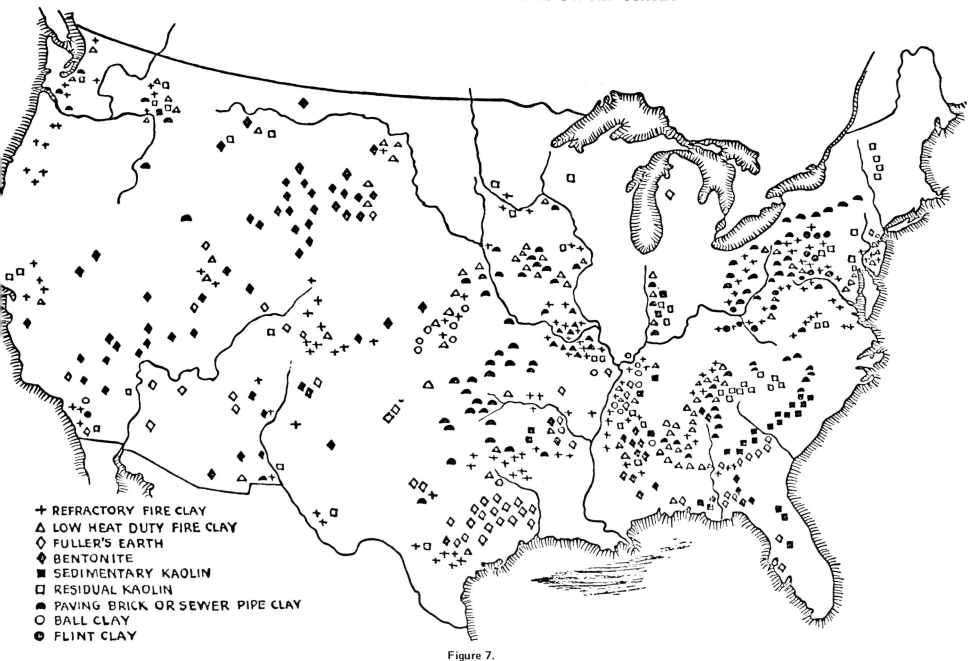

+ REFRACTORY FIRE CLAY
△ LOW HEAT DUTY FIRE CLAY
◇ FULLER'S EARTH
◈ BENTONITE
◼ SEDIMENTARY KAOLIN
▢ RESIDUAL KAOLIN
◖ PAVING BRICK OR SEWER PIPE CLAY
○ BALL CLAY
◉ FLINT CLAY

Figure 7.

Figure 8. One of the simplest ways to prospect for clay is to drive slowly along a highway observing the terrain and watching for road-cuts.

Figure 9. Typical cracking patterns of surface clay caused by weathering. The light particles are sandstone contaminations.

WHERE TO FIND CLAY

The idea that clay can only be acquired through purchase from dealers, that elaborate equipment and effort are needed, or that purchased clays are superior in quality are truly wrong. Clay is the most abundant material on earth. The advantages of the use of self-prepared local clay in the studio and in the classroom have been mentioned in the preceding paragraphs, but the most convincing argument for the use of one's own clay is its relative economy and abundant availability. Prospected clay costs almost nothing once the initial investment of a few buckets and sieves has been made.

Ruth M. Home has made an extensive study of clay resources of the world in her book CERAMICS FOR THE POTTER (Charles A. Bennett Company, U.S. Edition, Peoria, Illinois, 1952). In it she has furnished a map of clay resources in the United States, which indicates the general pattern of distribution throughout the country. Obviously no map could possibly indicate every individual deposit, but there are many which, though they may have no commercial value, could be useful in a small studio or school program. During a study undertaken at Texas Technological University in West Texas, an area known for its semi-arid character and sandy soils, the author over a period of two years located more than 25 large surface deposits. Eight of these deposits had commercial potential and literally hundreds of small ones were overlooked. Every one of these could have served for years as a clay pit for a small shop or a high school. This despite the fact that by geological standards West Texas has always been considered a "clay poor" area. In other words, the artist-potter and/or teacher should not attempt to look for commercially useful deposits unless they are already known and available. If they are, then their use is to be encouraged because they save time for the potter. Where such deposits do not exist, however, the potter should look for his own clay pit. He may be assured that, if he looks, he will find usable clay within a 25-mile radius almost anywhere in the United States.

One of the simplest ways to prospect for clay is to drive slowly along a highway observing the terrain and watching for road-cuts and outcroppings in the landscape. The edges of rivers and creeks are also likely places to look, and in hilly and mountainous regions river banks should become the first places to explore. In observing the general topography of the landscape, one should look for spots which have been exposed by erosion. Surface clays, once they have been found, are easily identified by their *cracking patterns.* These cracking patterns develop from the *slaking* properties of clay when it is exposed to the elements. Once these patterns are known to a person, they become obvious in nature and clays can readily be located. They can even be seen at some distance from a slow-moving vehicle.

The markings of useful clays should be strongly developed, pronounced, and deep. Weak patterns indicate greater soil and sand contamination of the clay and make it less desirable. Sands and soils never develop definite cracking patterns. Clays along river beds and creeks are usually moist and cracks are not visible. Such clays can be tested by drying out a small quantity in a shop and then checking for the patterns. When water is poured over such dry clay and then the latter allowed to dry, the pattern should develop. Another characteristic to look for in prospecting for clay at a distance is the presence of *wave-like* contours. Outcroppings in the landscape, often several hundred feet away, will reveal soft wave-like outlines against the horizon. These undulating outlines are caused by the *weathering* of the clay as it is exposed to rains. When such outcroppings are examined at close range, they reveal the same cracking patterns as mentioned before. Erosion often cuts away the top soil and exposes clays on the landscape. In drier regions of the country river beds may be good sources of clay. The clay particles carried down the river by spring waters have a tendency to settle at the bottom of pools as the water recedes. Once the river dries out, the clay forms a heavily cracked layer which can be lifted off and in quantity makes usable clay. More important, such pools indicate that clay may be further up the river. Clay can often be located wherever digging is occurring, such as in roadbuilding, house excavating, or pit digging.

When prospecting for clay, one should always have enough empty cartons, paper bags, or buckets at hand to collect enough

7

Figure 10. This familiar outcropping of surface clay reveals the wavelike, undulating contours of clay. Upon close inspection the typical cracking patterns can be recognized.

Figure 11. Formations of clay used in the studio of Clyde Burt along the Little Auglaize river in Paulding county, Ohio.

samples. A small shovel, a pick-axe, and a notebook for recording locations are also useful. The "turkey-size" plastic bags which are inexpensive, waterproof, and easy to carry are recommended.

Once a spot of earthy material has been found which could contain clay, it should be given an extremely simple finger test. From a small but very pure-looking sample of the material, form a small ball the size of a pea, lay it in the palm of the hand, and rub it with one's fingers. If the sample after the addition of a few drops of water feels "soapy" and sticky, then one is almost sure to have found usable clay.

Clay in larger deposits and in commercial quarries resembles a kind of soft rock. Often it has been deposited in layers called *strata.* When this is the case, the best place to obtain samples is where the "rock-shapes" seem most concentrated or packed. It should be emphasized, however, that even these clays when dried out and exposed to water will slake and eventually form the same cracks as surface deposits. This characteristic which is present in all clays is quite conspicuous at the edges of quarries.

HOW TO PREPARE CLAY

Once an ample amount of clay has been secured and tested from a *clay pit* or a surface deposit, the remaining clay can be processed for later use. This too is a simple process. The necessary equipment consisting of inexpensive tools that usually last several years can be assembled ahead of time:

1. Several three-gallon plastic buckets.

2. A sieve made from a discarded window-screen stretched over a 12 x 12-inch frame made from 1 x 4-inch lumber scraps.

3. A discarded 3 to 4-inch painter's brush. The shorter the bristles on the brush the better it will perform.

4. Several plaster bats: 14 x 16-inch plaster bats are best as they can readily be carried from one place to another. The bats should be at least one and one-half inches thick for good absorption.

Figure 12. Students at the Kyoto, Japan, College of Fine Arts coping with the problems of shaping clay. In most European and Asian schools students must learn to use local clays.

Figure 13. His thoughts are "CLAY." Master-potter John Kudlacek from Kansas.

All clay brought in from a pit must first be dried out. The time to dry out clay varies, some clays need several weeks. The clay should be poured out and spread on a sunny spot in the back of the studio and forgotten for two, or, three weeks. When clays are purchased in powder form then the drying-out process can be omitted. Once the clay has been dried out properly, it can be processed in the following way:

Step 1. Remove by hand most of the visible pebbles, twigs, and leaves from the clay. If the clay forms large lumps, break them up with a hammer.

Step 2. Fill several clean buckets with warm water and add enough dry clay to have the water stand approximately one inch above the clay.

Step 3. Next day stir the clay well, adding water if necessary to form a *slip*. Slip is clay in liquid form. The consistency of the slip should be such as to enable the clay to be worked through the sieve into a clean bucket. The best consistency is achieved when the slip pours like "coffee-cream."

Step 4. The clay is then poured and worked through the sieve with the aid of the brush. This action removes any sand and foreign matter that may have remained. More importantly, it provides a vigorous *mixing action* by sifting the clay and aiding in the uniform distribution of the clay particles.

Step 5. The buckets filled with the sifted clay are again left to stand and settle over night. Next day the excess water may be syphoned off and the remaining thick slip poured upon the dry plaster bats. The plaster will absorb any excess of water from the clay and leave the plastic *clay cakes* for use. After several hours on the bats the clay cakes are ready for wedging. Many craftsmen shy away from the use of plaster bats because of the possibility of the clay being contaminated, instead of plaster bats, burlap can be spread on concrete, or thick layers of old newspapers spread on a concrete floor will serve the same purpose, when using old papers, top the layer with burlap, otherwise the clay will adhere to the paper.

Figure 14. Master potter Jerry Rothman demonstrating the construction of scaffolds to make giant, ceramic forms. Over 300 potters from all parts of the country attended this Ceramic Conference on the campus of the State University of Pennsylvania at College Station.

Figure 15. Artist Herta Hillfon from Stockholm, Sweden, proves convincingly that clay can be made to look like "anything." Unglazed earthenware, 45 x 25 x 30 centimeters, 1972.

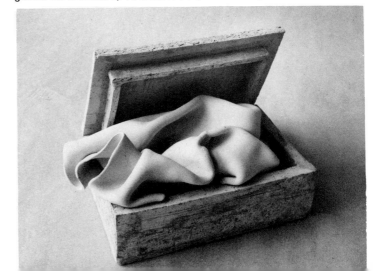

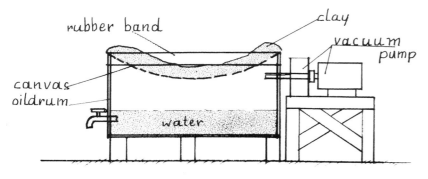

Figure 16. A vacuum filter bat can remove excess moisture from 40 to 50 pounds of clay at one pouring.

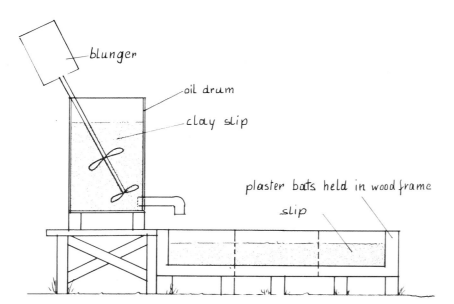

Figure 17. Combination clay assembly as used by many potteries in Europe and in Asia.

The foregoing description should be recognized as the simplest possible process of clay preparation for any meaningful work and is recommended only on a small scale for classroom use or within a one-man studio. Once any permanent or consistent production is planned, the preparation of an individualized clay-body must be considered from many points of view. Often the artist-potter dislikes the effort and time he must spend in preparing clay because he considers it dead work which contributes little to his creative genius. This is an illusion, however, which I hope has been amply explained and hopefully eliminated in previous paragraphs. Many master-potters of the past and present have given extreme care and love to the preparation of their clays, and have looked upon their material as the foundation of their art form. On the continent of Europe, clay preparation is always placed in the charge of trusted people and carefully supervised.

Several ways exist for preparing clay on a large scale without great investment:

A *Vacuum Filter Bat* can remove the excess moisture from 40 to 50 pounds of clay at one pouring. It needs no drying-out as plaster bats do between uses, and is simple to construct. A metal 200-gallon drum is cut by a welder at both ends to form two containers about 12 inches high, with the middle discarded. Heavy canvas is stretched over the top, and a hose leading to a vacuum pump is connected to the bat through a nipple below the canvas. The slip when poured upon the canvas will close the pores. As a slight vacuum is created in the tub, suction occurs and the water is drawn out of the clay into the barrel. Clay cakes can be removed usually after 30 to 40 minutes and the bat used immediately. The author has seen such a canvas-bat used in a Swedish pottery plant producing more than 200 pounds of clay per day.

Many self-employed artist-potters in Europe prepare their bodies in slip form in large floatation bats. These artists, after testing their clays, adhere strictly to their own formulas. Such are the Trillers in Sweden. In their two-man shop in Tobo, Sweden, Ingrid and Erik Triller add love and care to their clay. After stirring the ingredients for hours with motorized equipment, the Trillers use a filter press. In smaller shops, vacuum bats could be used with success.

Figure 18. Parts for the pugmill. (1) Ejection assembly consisting of a 2 1/2-inch nipple, bell reducer to 1 1/2 inch, and a 1 1/2-inch female plug. (2) 5/8 bearings with retaining rings. (3) 3-inch washer. (4) Sprockets with double link chains for direct drive from motor. (5) SKF-F40 pillowblocks. (6) Lower part of the auger.

Figure 19. The auger has been obtained from a 3-inch transport, such as are used in grain elevators. The lower part of the auger has been cut with a torch at three inch intervals to increase its mixing action. The part covered by the auger housing has no cuts and the blades primarily function to transport, and to compress the clay into the ejection assembly.

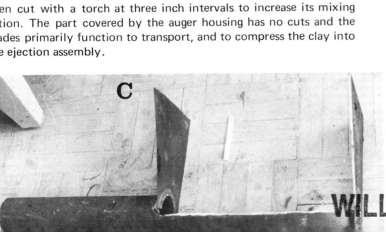

Figure 20. The pugmill feeder housing before the attachment of the side plates.

There are several different ways plaster bats can be used for the removal of excess water from clay slips. One method is to sandwich clay slips between a series of bats. This uses the absorbing quality of both sides of the bat simultaneously. While this method speeds the drying-out of the clay, the bats cannot be used in succession without thorough drying of the bats between uses. Very practical for smaller studios are a number of *bowl-shaped* bats which are readily made from two plastic dish bowls of varying sizes. The plaster in liquid form is poured into the larger bowl, after which the smaller bowl is pressed gently into the setting plaster and, if necessary weighed down with a brick. When the plaster has set, the plastic bowls are easily removed and plaster-bowls result. Another very practical way to prepare clay for a small-scale production is a combination of the barrel and bat method. This set-up saves much time when there is enough space to construct it on a permanent basis. (Such a structure can often be seen in family potteries in Europe and a similar unit can be found in Bernard Leach's *Potters' Book*—indicating that this method is apparently used also in the Orient.) When such a clay trough is constructed, one should mount it at least 6 to 10 inches above the ground in order to aid bottom ventilation, and then line the trough with cheap cotton material to aid in the removal of the heavy slip. The trough system does not produce clay that is sufficiently plastic and the "cakes" taken from the trough by lifting the ends of the lining usually have to be wedged to the right consistency on dry wedging bats. The benefit of the trough is that it produces a larger amount of very heavy slip. This very soft plastic clay must then undergo the finishing process on another dry bat or wedging table.

Despite the foregoing, it is necessary to point out that most studio-potters would prefer to own a workable *pugmill*. There are a number of different clay-mixing machines available on the market which would fit into the artist's studio, but few if any do the job he needs to have done. Most mixers prepare clay only partially. The equipment coming closest to producing a clay mixture which could immediately be used for production without undergoing any interim steps is a pugmill. At this time the author knows of only one workable pugmill which has been designed for

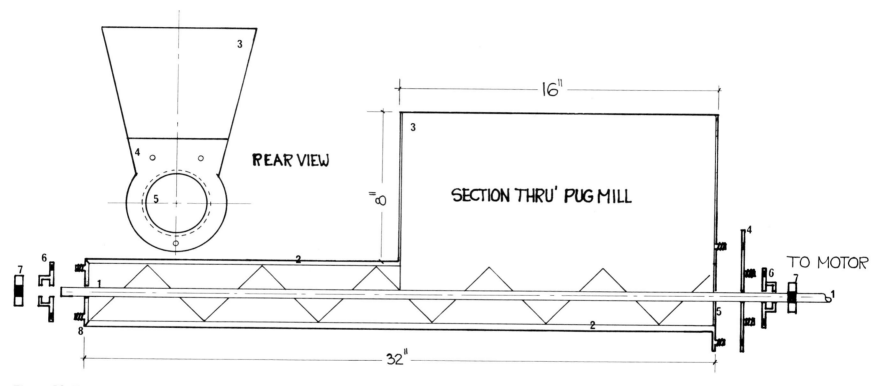

Figure 21. This pugmill has been constructed from scrap materials and the overall cost in 1969 did not exceed $50.00. Section through the pugmill: (1) auger; (2) 3-inch pipe; (3) feeder housing through which auger can be removed; (4) shaft retaining plate, removable if necessary for auger repairs and cleaning; (5) opening in feeder housing through which auger can be removed; (6) 5/8 bearings held in place with SKF-F40 pillowblocks; (7) retaining rings for bearings; (8) 3-inch washer.

the artist-potter's use and which would not pinch his budget. The precision and power required in the construction of a pugmill usually stop the attempts of many artist-potters and of schools to build their own. The pugmill presented here was constructed with the help of a student assistant who knew how to weld. However, if one assumes that the cost of a welder would have to be added, the amount needed to construct this pugmill would still be minimal. In 1972 it was $50.00. New parts cost $28.25, and slightly more than four hours of time were required to construct the mill. Except for the bearings, pillowblocks, sprockets, and a few bolts, all materials were purchased from a scrap metal dealer at the price of five cents a pound. A 3-inch transport from a grain elevator was used for the auger, and a piece of 3-inch black pipe for the auger-housing. The body of the mill was welded from 3/16's sheet metal. These materials can be cheaply acquired throughout the country wherever farm industry is found. To power the pugmill properly, a used electric elevator motor with a gear reduction to 30 RPM was attached.

The pugmill mixes and prepares approximately 200 pounds of clay per hour. It serves most efficiently when the clay has been premoistened and fed into the mill along with dry clay powder to achieve the desired consistency. Ceramic bodies are best premixed in dry state in buckets or by the use of a small used "concrete mixer." They can then be dampened over night in large containers by the addition of approximately 40 percent of water. Each clay varies as to the amount of water of plasticity and only one's experience can establish the exact amount of water needed. The water is best poured between layers of dry clay-powder. When all clay has been added, the mix should be covered with rags and the remaining water poured over it. More water may also be added during the pugging until the right consistency has been achieved. The clay leaves the pugmill ready for use. The author uses the pugmill in the following way. He usually pugs a larger amount of clay at one time and stores it for aging in several plastic trash cans which can be purchased in discount stores. After a period of several weeks, he processes the aged clay once more through the mill to improve its consistency before throwing on the wheel. This

Figure 22. Detail showing the attachment of the ejection assembly and the three-inch washer. The bolts are welded to the washer. The washer forms the front plate of the pugmill and functions as the base for the bearings.

Figure 23. The pugmill in action. Pre-moistened clay is shown in the shallow pan and dry-mix in the bucket. The motor is a used, 1/2 horse power, elevator motor with a gear reduction to 30 RPM's. The motor was purchased from an Army Surplus Store. A piece of hardwood serves as the stoker.

almost eliminates any elaborate wedging. Although no de-airing of the clay can be claimed, the clay is usually packed enough in the ejection assembly of the pugmill to be free of damaging air bubbles.

HOW TO TEST CLAYS

The physical properties of clay can be defined as its *plasticity, fusibility, color, texture, tensile strength, shrinkage, slaking property, absorption,* and *specific gravity.* From this list the most important for the artist-potter to know within his limited uses in a small-scale production are: plasticity, fusibility, color, texture, and shrinkage—in that order.

Plasticity can be defined as *fat* (high plasticity) or *lean* (low plasticity). Sand in the clay decreases its plasticity and when present in excess makes clay unusable. Plasticity can be tested simply by rolling out a coil of clay about the size of a pencil and winding it around one's finger. Good plastic clay will show no cracks, lean clay will reveal cracks or break apart entirely.

Fusibility indicates the changes occurring in clay during the firing—namely the firing shrinkage, volatilization of some of the components, and density of the clay. The maturing temperature of a clay can be determined by fusibility tests. A simple way to carry out these tests is to form several cones of the clay approximately three-fourths of an inch thick at the base and four inches high, and submit these to firings at different temperatures. For example, fire one cone 04, another to cone 1, and another to cone 4, and so on until the final cone indicates some deformation. Be sure to place the cones in the kiln on a piece of old shelfing or brick to avoid damaging the shelves in case the clay should melt badly. Some clays will not withstand cone 8 and will deform, others at this temperature may show a dense hard surface which is difficult to scratch, and still others may stay porous and absorb an excessive amount of water. A water absorption of 3 to 5 percent indicates the approximate ideal maturing temperature for stoneware bodies. In that connection, the water of absorption can be tested by weighing accurately the fired but unglazed piece, then submerging it in water for at least three hours—after which time it is removed

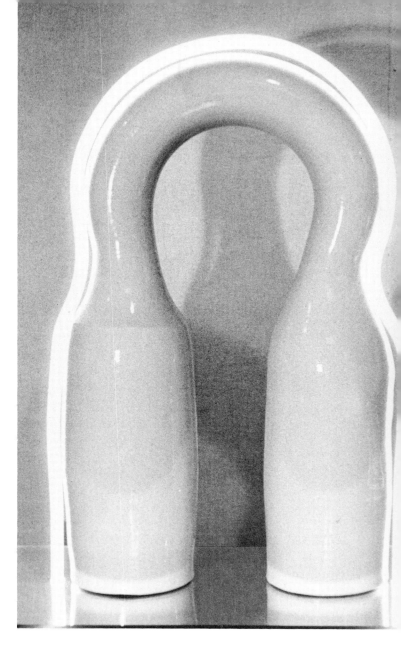

Figure 24. Clay and Neon, by Bill Farrell, Illinois, stoneware, 24 inches high.

from the water, lightly dried off, and weighed again. The difference in weight is the absorption factor.

The *color* of clay will change with the firing temperature. A good time to register the color of certain clays is presented during the fusibility tests when the color of one particular clay can be seen when exposed to different temperatures.

The *texture* of clays depends primarily upon the presence in the clay-body of coarse aggregates. In natural clay this may be silica in the form of sand. Aggregates can also be added to clays when more texture is desired. In tests for shrinkage and fusibility these aggregates should be incorporated into the body as they affect both. The particular aggregate, sand, or grog is kneaded into a small amount of clay and test tiles are formed. The best size for test tiles is 3 x 3 inches plus one-half inch thickness.

All clays shrink during the drying and firing process. The *air-shrinkage* takes place during the drying of the piece and before it has been subjected to extreme heat. Workable clay contains 35 percent to 45 percent of water for plasticity. The evaporation of this water causes a drawing together of the clay particles, which in turn causes the piece to shrink. Even after the air-shrinkage ceases, a small percentage of the water remains in the clay. This can be driven off only by heating the piece at approximately 200 degrees Fahrenheit for several hours. Lean clays shrink considerably less than highly plastic clays.

The *firing-shrinkage* is usually determined by the quantities of *combined water, organic matter,* and *carbon dioxide* in the body. These are called the *volatile elements* of a clay. Shrinkage is further influenced by the temperature the clay has been exposed to during the firing, and the ratio of fluxes in the clay. The firing-shrinkage of clays has been found to be from two percent to an excess of 12 percent. In the latter case, pieces usually come out warped and deformed.

Shrinkage tests should be carried out with every clay one intends to use in the studio. The simplest way to check a clay for shrinkage is by forming a test tile with the following dimensions: 12 centimeters long, 5 centimeters wide, and 1 centimeter thick. With a ruler the tile is marked as shown in the illustration. The tile is then measured after drying, and again after the final

15

Figure 25. Traditional Japanese potter making large pots by the *thrown-coil* method: large coils are added to the dried lower section and adjoined by hand, then the wheel is kicked by foot, water is added for easier throwing . . . .

Figure 26. . . . and the wall is quickly thrown thin and even. Ottani pottery, Japan.

Figure 27. Stoneware sculpture by Charles J. Fager, University of South Florida.

firing to its maturing temperature. The difference in length between each stage indicates the shrinkage between each stage. Measurements in centimeters are recommended because, if the basic mark on the fresh clay is 10 centimeters (100 millimeters), then the shrinkage can immediately and easily be translated into a *percentage* of shrinkage.

Often brickyards and clay factories provide charts of the physical characteristics of nearby clays. In such cases much of the testing can be avoided by a study of these charts. The following is a sample of a chart showing typical physical properties. As these vary with every clay, only a few have been selected to demonstrate the possibility of interpretation of facts as they would apply in their use by an artist-potter.

Physical Properties of Clays

Location	Slak-ing	Plasti-city	Drying Shrink. (%)	Firing* Shrink. (%)	Color	Water of Absorp-tion (%)
Post, Carza Co., Tex.	fast	moder-ate	4.7	2.6	wh	12.5
Silverton, Colo.	mod.	high	6.7	4.2	red	4.5
Sargent Bluff, Ia.	mod.	v. high	7.2	3.8	brown	6.0

*—All samples have been fired to cone 1.

Figure 28. Test tile to measure clay shrinkage.

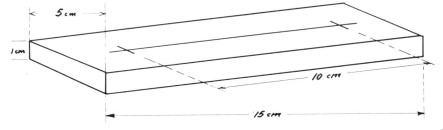

Such charts are usually published on a state or county basis by the clay industry or are included in geological surveys published by state governments. The interpretation of facts useful to the artist-potter proceeds along the following lines: Highly *plastic* clays are good for throwing on the potter's wheel; on the other hand, they are less suitable for casting and pressing processes. A fast *slaking* clay almost always indicates a poor plasticity; with the slowing of the slaking process, however, plasticity usually increases. Coarse sandy clays usually slake in an instant. A high percentage of *air-shrinkage* usually indicates the danger of cracking in the drying process. Clays with an air-shrinkage of four percent to six percent are considered normal and will perform well in the usual sun-drying. Clays with a high percentage of shrinkage should be dried very slowly: if necessary, the pieces should be covered during the initial stages of drying to retard the speed of water evaporation. The *water of absorption* factor allows for at least two deductions to be made. First, a very high rate of absorption indicates a very porous body, which in turn opens the possibility of testing the body at higher temperatures. This also usually indicates an underfired clay. In some cases, such as in ovenware, this may be the desired result because very loose bodies are more resistant to heat shock. Second, a very low absorption rate may mean a highly fused body which in this case may be brittle and easily breakable.

IMPROVING CLAYS

The term *clay* as used thus far has been defined as an earthy material found in nature without the addition of any other material. When a number of clays or ceramic chemicals are combined for the purpose of forming a special clay, they are called a *clay-body*. When improvements on simple clays are accomplished by the addition of some other clay, then the mixture too becomes a clay-body and ceases to be clay only. The term "improvement" as used here again implies a basic change in the composition of the original clay. The number of ways a clay can be changed is rather limited. For our purposes clays can be changed only in four ways, which include changing the:

1. plasticity of a clay-body

2. maturing temperature (fusibility)

3. color

4. texture

The plasticity of any simple clay can be improved by an addition of other known plastic clays in percentages up to 50 percent.

Figure 29. Clay is an amazing and versatile medium. Sheldon Carey throwing large cylinders upside-down in his University of Kansas studio. Mr. Carey invented and constructed the upside-down wheel he is working on.

Figure 30. Sand molded stoneware mural for Nacka Hospital, Sweden, by Stig Lindberg.

Figure 31. Don Reitz, the Wisconsin master-potter throwing one of his giant pots.

Figure 32. Kenji Kato, from the Tajimi pottery in Japan, demonstrating *throwing from the hump* during a visit in the United States.

Bentonite added to a clay-body in small amounts of one percent to a maximum of two percent will also improve the plasticity. Perhaps the most practical and common way to improve the plasticity of clays can be achieved by an addition of 5 percent to 25 percent of any *ball clay*. Ball clays, as has been stated before, have an extremely small particle size which aids the plasticity significantly. The introduction of ball clay into a clay-body will also raise its fusibility, making the clay available at higher temperatures. In reverse the plasticity of a clay can be decreased by the addition of *Kaolins*, or potters' flint, which is a fine form of silica. The addition of *Grog* (which is ground, fired, fire clay) or as much as 15 percent or less of fine builders' sand, will also considerably shorten any clay. All these additives are basically of the same chemical composition. These materials should first be added to test tiles in small quantities and then increased as necessary after continuous testing. Any addition of refractory materials will automatically raise the maturing temperature of a clay-body; therefore *line-tests* with additions of five percent at each step are recommended for those who desire to develop an ideal clay-body from local clays.

To change the color of a clay, small amounts of color oxides can be introduced. Most ceramic literature contains complete charts showing the amounts of oxides to be added to achieve desired colors. The writer's point of view in the use of coloring bodies is simple. Unless some very special reasons exist for doing otherwise, exploit the natural color of the clay. *Iron oxide* is the most commonly used colorant for clays. Used in small percentages of 1 percent to 3 percent, it often enhances the warmth of a clay-body. A one-half percent of cobalt oxide will produce a wide variety of greys, blue-greys, and black—depending upon the original color of the clay.

The texture of clay-bodies can be changed by an addition of aggregates, the most common of which are *grog* and *sand*. For sculptural bodies or large pieces which will have walls exceeding one inch in thickness, an addition of up to 50 percent of grog is not uncommon. For wheel work the grog should be fine or approximately 30 mesh. When builders' sand is used in a clay, care should be taken that all foreign matter such as leaves and sticks have been removed, for even small pieces of such materials may later cause cracking.

It is safe to say that in general any addition of materials to a clay will affect all four criteria of change. To some degree plasticity, fusibility, color, and texture will all be affected and only meaningful testing with accurate recording will result in a desired clay-body.

It is also a general rule that one of the most important improvements which will enhance the over-all workability of freshly prepared clay is the *aging* of the clay-body. This cannot be emphasized strongly enough. In the author's experience, the aging factor is grossly overlooked by many artist-potters—and even more so in educational plants. Pottery plants in the past have aged their clays for months and months because this was the only known way to improve the maleable qualities of their materials. In the Orient, the aging process often took a generation, while in Italy bits of old blankets were mixed and wedged into the clay so that its decomposition would aid the plasticity. To age a clay effectively one has to remember that clay will "age" only after it has first been *wedged*. Clay will not improve when stored in slip or dry form. It must have gone through the wedging process (during which an intimate and perfect distribution of the clay particles has been established) before its decomposition will significantly aid the clay-body. This wedging can be performed by hand or by a pug-mill. After aging and before use, a clay should be reworked slightly to improve its consistency.

TYPES OF CLAY

Common red clays can be defined as various *surface clays* containing a wide range of soil or sand contamination. While such clays are not pure enough to be used in clay industries, they can be used in the limited programs of potteries, studios, and classrooms. They are most abundantly found everywhere in the United States, and their primary use is in the production of lesser art wares, flowerpots, and some brickyards. Many of the common red clays lend themselves to structural improvements by the addition

Figure 33. Church in Savona, Italy, by Nino Caruso. Modular wall elements, white matt glaze, the positive and negative relief allows for a rich and changeable texture.

Figure 34. Donc Series, by Henry Cabaniss, University of Texas, earthenware, 48 inches high, cone 1 glaze, black, with black and white platinum on the glaze.

Figure 35. From the "Ceramic Garden," by John Kudlacek, Kansas. Indeed, the forms of clay are sprouting through the snow announcing new life to come.

of other clays. Their deposits in the landscape may vary from a small hole in a sandy soil to commercial quarries only two to five feet below the top soil.

Red firing stoneware and *plastic* clays are suitable for use at higher temperatures and therefore are usable for a wider range of products such as roofing and other tiles, sewer pipes, industrial stoneware, crockery, art ware, patio ware, and so on. These clays are ideal for the studio-potter to use in modeling and throwing on the potter's wheel. Many of the buff-burning clays should be included in this category. They are important, and some of the best stoneware bodies have developed from them in combination with less plastic fire clays. The most famous natural stoneware clays in the United States are Jordan and Monmouth clays.

White plastic clays, kaolins, and *fire clays* have their color in common but vary widely in other physical properties. Wherever these clays are available to the artist-potter, they are a welcome additive to his clay-bodies. The highly plastic ball clays are also part of this group and are usually used in the composition of porcelain bodies. Most of these clays are mined and can be obtained through ceramic dealers.

Chapter II

New Concepts in Glazes

Figure 36. Kenji Kato, stoneware vase with wax resist decoration and a temmoku glaze fired in a heavy oil kiln to cone 10 in 12 1/2 hours.

THE NATURE OF GLAZES

Glazes are made from clays. They consist of three parts: fluxes, alumina, and silicates, which form the glassy cover over a piece of ceramics. In ceramic chemistry these are divided into three distinct groups (according to their oxygen relationships) known as monoxide, dioxide, or trioxide compounds. The chemical symbols for these groups are expressed as the RO - R_2O_3 - and RO_2 factors. *Each component has its own fuction within the glaze.* The fluxes determine the maturing temperature of the glaze batch, and strongly influence its textural appearance and colors. The alumina, usually added to glazes in the form of various clays, is the refractory component whose main function is to keep the glaze from running off the pot during the melting process. The silica, added usually in the form of potters' flint or ground quartz, is the "glass former" in the glaze. By itself, silica is highly refractory and has a melting point higher than 3,000 degrees Fahrenheit, but in combination with fluxes its melting temperature is brought well within the firing ranges of most studio potters.

The original purpose for glazes was to make a piece impervious. In our time, in the age of conceptual pottery, this utilitarian purpose for glazes has become relatively insignificant. Glazes are now primarily appreciated for their aesthetic qualities. Their textures, colors, and other effects, which are created by their interaction with body-clays when submitted to extremely high heat, add a sophistication and beauty to the clay which it may otherwise have

Figure 37. Potter Jim Cantrell glazing the inside of a bowl.

Figure 38. Kenneth Fergusson, Kansas City Art Institute. Raku jar covered with a thick crackle glaze with smoke effects.

lacked. For this reason alone, glazes in the past have been regarded as closely-kept secrets. But today glazes have become the fascination of the creative studio-potter. Small subtle changes in the amounts of the various materials can make a noticeable change in the appearance of a final glaze. In effect, changes may render a glaze beautiful or monotonous—or a shiny piece of lost work. The desire, then, to develop individualized reliable glazes keeps both amateurs and professionals experimenting. For many, however, experimentation involves no more than the mixing together of leftover glaze scraps and the application of the mixture upon a "last" pot before closing the kiln door. At times, when such experiments succeed, the results can seldom be duplicated because of the haphazard approach of the experimenter. Others go to much effort to master and understand the laws of glaze chemistry and make empirical calculations in order to "create" their own glaze formulas. For the most part, they soon discover, as this writer has, that within studio limits, the results are hardly worth the effort. While their glazes may have perfect chemical balance and melt smoothly, they usually lack excitement and life. The particular effects and interesting variations in tone, color, and texture, which the potter seeks (or the very things which make a glaze desirable) are usually caused by small minute imbalances in chemistry and by the impurities of many materials. After all, the great wealth of the most desirable and admired ceramic pieces were created, glazed, and fired before chemistry was a science. From Egypt, China, and India came some of the most fascinating glazes in the history of ceramics, and the people who produced them had no "perfect" kilns, spray-guns, ball-mills, nor did they have a scientific knowledge of chemistry. The complexity of the glazing process, considering fuel, gasses, interaction of the chemicals with heat, oxidizing or reducing atmospheres, all tend to make glazing less than a strictly scientific process. But a common sense approach and desire to learn will bring the beginner far on the way to success, and his achievement will be enhanced by genuine inquiry. Strictly technical data and information needed for the advanced ceramist, or the ceramic engineer, are amply available in specialized literature.

The chemistry of glazes has its laws of reactions and balances. These chemical balances are important and must be considered if good glazes are to result. Nevertheless, it has been generally known for a long time that, within the studio-potter's realm, decimals and fractions of chemicals could be avoided without seriously impeding the final appearance of glazes. The implication of such a statement, which is usually justified for reasons of "ease of calculations," is clearly that there are margins and tolerances within a glaze formula. These tolerances will be important later in this chapter as we consider conversions and composition of glazes.

The following discussion of glazes is based upon two important observations: first, that the great majority of beginners and advanced studio-potters would rather change glaze formulas to suit their particular needs than to design their "own" glazes (such formulas are readily available in quantity in standard ceramic literature); and second, it is important for the studio-potter to be able to perform these conversions properly, meaningfully, and successfully. Therefore, the emphasis has not been placed upon calculations and development of new glaze formulas, although this is a part of the study, but rather upon the ability to change glazes meaningfully in order to achieve specifically desired glaze effects.

A large part of success depends upon organized testing and recording of experiments. The importance of accurate recording of experimental results cannot be stressed enough. This practice preserves many good glaze formulas for later uses, but more than that the glaze records themselves will form a notebook which in a short period of time will provide the student with more experience, knowledge, and know-how in glazemaking than any text could ever offer. A 5 x 7 inch filing card which is used by the author for testing and glaze-filing purposes is indicated in the illustration. When using a notebook, the author considers a bound leaf book the best insurance against lost pages. But generally it can be stated that any filing system will suffice; the important thing is its accuracy and consistency.

Technically, glazes are divided into several types, a knowledge of which will greatly benefit the experimenter. The typifications of glazes vary with different writers and some derive their names

Figure 39. Stoneware figures by Lisa Larson, Sweden.

Figure 40. Glazing can often be a simple, common sense process, provided the potter has knowledge of the effects particular compounds will have on the molten glaze. Above the author observing Paul Soldner preparing glazes for a raku demonstration at the campus of Texas Tech University.

Figure 41. The Swedish ceramist Lisa Larson well known throughout Europe for her humorous figures and stoneware pots.

Figure 42. Kurt Ohnsorg, Vienna, Austria. Two slab built pieces with heavily applied, buttery, magnesium glaze.

from special characteristics or places of manufacture, such as the Bristol type or aventurine glazes. In this study, three factors of classification are more prominent than others. First, the maturing temperature of the glaze; second, the base flux of the glaze; and third, the preparation of the glaze. These types of glazes are:

1. High Fire Glazes
2. Low Fire Glazes
3. Lead Glazes
4. Lead Free Glazes
5. Raw Glazes
6. Fritted Glazes

Any single glaze can be fitted in this system. For example, a typical cone 04 glossy glaze can be classified as a Low Fire, Raw, Lead glaze; and any stoneware glaze may be a High Fire, Raw, Leadless glaze. Such classification will simplify the records of glaze-making when accurately used.

Before advancing to the changing and compounding of glazes, one more set of general rules should be noted:

1. Know the basic functions of your glaze materials well. They are described under the *Characteristics of Basic Glaze Materials* at the end of this chapter.

2. Know that the better the glaze materials are intermixed in the glaze-batch, the better will they melt to form a uniform glaze during the firing process.

3. Know that glazes consist of three components, the fluxes, the refractories (clay), and the silica (glass-former).

4. Know that the appearance of any glaze can be changed by conversion of one or more components in the glaze batch.

CHANGING GLAZES

As has been established before, the studio potter's glazes are simple mixtures of refined clays and chemicals which can be

24

changed. Many of the materials can be purchased locally, but all of them are available from ceramic supply houses at a very reasonable cost. For several reasons, the use of local clays in glazes is almost always beneficial. Local clays affect the fitting of the glaze to the clay-body, and grazing seldom occurs. They also individualize the glaze in terms of surface texture and color. The effects produced in a glaze by the introduction of local clay cannot be duplicated by other potters because of the specific chemical composition of the clay in that particular locality. And finally, the use of local materials reduces the cost of making glazes to such low levels that there can be no justification for purchasing prepared, commercial products. Based on a pound of glaze, the cost is approximately one-tenth that of a commmercial glaze.

The idea of developing new glazes from an existing "glaze formula" by systematically changing some of its conponents is not new. This is exactly what the ceramic engineer does with the aid of glaze chemistry. This approach may be designated as the *Parts-by-Weight* system. It emphasizes the fact that one is dealing with parts-by-weight, which is essential to the system. **The "system" rests upon the simplified use of molecular equivalents of ceramic materials. The *PbW* units in the study simply correspond to 0.10 units, or batch-weights of a particular chemical.**

This simplification almost amounted to a revolution in glaze-making when it was introduced several years ago to classes of beginning and advanced students of ceramics. Usually, beginning students tend to be puzzled by an introduction to normal glaze chemistry. Ninety percent of the students exposed to the *PbW* system recorded real successes so quickly that they even surprised themselves. When the rules for changing glazes were presented in simple terms and weights, the students responded enthusiastically and felt inspired to do their best. The ease with which glazes could be changed and new glazes developed made the course a creative experience for the participants.

To "exchange" implies the substitution of one glaze material for another: upon this principle lies the chemical balance of the glaze. The following conversions in the tables below are such substitutions. They are presented in this study in the form of statements of how to accomplish the same thing a ceramic engineer

Figure 43. Master potter Richard Peeler from the University of Indiana examining one of his applique pots.

Figure 44. The shiny lids on salt glazed pots of potter Tom Collins appear like flying saucers in the dawn.

Ten Rules for Changing Glazes

WHEN REMOVING:	PbW	ADD:	PbW
Rule #1			
Silica (flint) may be added or removed without regard to other materials in the glaze batch. Approximately 30 PbW of flint will increase the maturing temperature by one cone.			
Rule #2			
White Lead	26	One of the following:	
		Whiting	10
		Zinc Oxide	8
		Barium Carbonate	20
Rule #3			
Whiting	10	One of the following:	
		White Lead	26
		Zinc Oxide	8
		Barium Carbonate	20
Rule #4			
Zinc Oxide	8	One of the following:	
		White Lead	26
		Whiting	10
		Barium Carbonate	20
Rule #5			
Barium Carbonate	20	One of the following:	
		White Lead	26
		Whiting	10
		Zinc Oxide	8
Rule #6			
Clay: local clay / kaolin / ball clay	26	silica (flint)	12
Rule #7			
Potash Feldspar	56	clay	26
		flint	24
		One of the following:	
		White Lead	26
		Whiting	10
or any PbW unit of flux from the conversion table on page			
WHEN ADDING:	PbW	**REMOVE:**	PbW
Rule #8			
Potash Feldspar	56	clay	26
		flint	24
		One of the following:	
		White Lead	26
		Whiting	10
or any PbW unit of flux from the conversion table on page			
Rule #9			
Clay: local clay / kaolin / ball clay	12	silica (flint)	12 / 12
Rule #10			
All glaze ingredients are interchangeable on a PbW basis when the above rules are followed. For example, 26 parts of white lead can also be replaced by: 38 parts of borax or by 18.5 parts of dolomite, etc.			

Figure 45. Glaze changing rules.

would do through chemistry. For example, a glossy bright glaze can be turned into a matte glaze by the removal of flint, according to Rule #1, but enough flint must remain in the formula to maintain the glass-making capacity of the glaze. Ball clay may also be added by Rule #9, substituting whiting at the expense of white lead by Rule #2. Illustration presents such a conversion from a typical glossy cone 04 lead glaze to a rich-looking matte.

To study the possibilities of this system, let us use as an example a low-fire, raw, lead glaze. The batch formula of this glaze is as follows:

White Lead	459
Whiting	60
Potash feldspar	313
Talc	18
Flint	119

1. Possibility: If the glaze seems to run excessively and a higher maturing temperature is desired, 15 or 30 PbW of flint added to the glaze according to Rule #1 would tend to offset the running defect.

2. Possibility: If more crystallization effects are desired in the gloss of the glaze, experiments could include: (a) the substitution of whiting for the zinc oxide according to Rule #3; or (b) the substitution of silica by Rule #1 according to the conversion tables; or (c) both of these exchanges.

3. Possibility: If more of a matte surface is desired, the procedure would be: (a) removal of flint by Rule #1; (b) the addition of clay by Rule #9; and (c) the substitution of whiting for white lead by Rule #2. This means:

For a more effective change in this glaze change multiples of the PbW-units of each compound are used. In practice: (a) Remove 4x6PbW of Flint = 24 PbW of flint. (b) Add 4x12PbW of clay = 48 PbW of clay substance. (c) Remove 4x26PbW of White Lead = 104 PbW of Wh. Lead. (c) Add 4x10PbW of Whiting = 40 PbW of Whiting.

In this glaze change, multiples of PbW units have been used. It should be perfectly obvious that refractions of multiples of PbW

26

Conversion Table for Basic Glaze Materials		Recommended Limits in Percentages
MATERIAL	PbW	PERCENT
Barium carbonate	20	0-30
Boric acid	13	
Borax	38	
Clay, ball	12	
Colemanite	41	0-50
Cornwall stone	82	
Dolomite	19	0-20
Feldspar, potash	56	
Feldspar, soda	53	
Kaolin	26	
Kaolin, calcined	22	
Flint	6	
Lead, white	12	
Lead, red	23	
Magnes, carb.	8	0-10
Nepheline syen.	46	
Soda Bicarb.	17	0-50
Soda Ash	11	
Titanium diox. (rutile)	8	0-12
Zinc oxide	8	0-40

Figure 46. Parts by weight conversion tables.

units require proportionate changes in the other values listed. The following are the three glaze batch-formulas after the changes have been completed.

Possibility #1 now appears this way:

White lead	459
Whiting	60
Feldspar	313
Talc	18
Flint	149

Possibility #2 now appears this way:

White lead	459
Whiting	40
Zinc oxide	16
Feldspar	313
Talc	18
Flint	119

Possibility #3 now appears this way:

White lead	355
Whiting	100
Feldspar	313
Kaolin	52
Talc	18
Flint	95
Clay	52

During the past few years, caused by a concern for the environment, the damaging effects of lead upon human health have been brought to the foreground. As a result lead containing glazes became unpopular. Most potters realize the concern is well founded, although exaggerated in some quarters. The P.b.W. (Parts by Weight) system, therefore, can also be used effectively to change any lead containing glaze into a *lead-less* glaze. For example, the flux in the above mentioned glaze can be replaced by *one* or, by several non-lead fluxing compounds.

Such a new glaze batch may look like this:

Possibility #4 (elimination of lead as flux).

Colmanite	717 (replacing 459 of wh. lead).
Whiting	60
Feldspar	313
Talc	18
Flint	119

A whole new series of usable glazes can be developed from this one basic change. By using a combination of low-fire fluxes as, dolomite, gerstley borate, and magnesium and sodium compounds new color, and textural possibilities develop.

For whatever purpose the P.b.W. system is used, one cardinal

Figure 47. Lauren C. Harper, U.S. Procelain jar with heavy, flowing glaze enhanced with a large copper red spot.

Figure 48. Artist-potter Ron Meyers and students in the glazing area of the ceramics department of the University of South Carolina.

rule must be observed, the whole system depends upon this adherance; EXCHANGE ONLY FLUXES WITH OTHER FLUXES, CLAYS WITH CLAYS, AND ACIDS WITH ACIDS. When this harmony of compounds is preserved thy possibilities to change glazes are almost unlimited. Using any formula, for any source, for any firing temperature, the limits are set only by the imagination of the experimenter. In theory and practice this system of changing glazes can achieve any change desired.

COMPOUNDING NEW GLAZES

Actually any glaze that has been changed by the PbW system in one or more of its components becomes a new glaze, for it will have a new texture, a new light and color refraction—or, in other words, a new life of its own. In reality, then, a way of making new glazes has already been discussed in depth and applied as the reader went about changing and adjusting his old glaze formulas. Here it is worth noting that most potteries in European countries possess a wealth of fine glaze formulas which excel in their simplicity. Most have been developed over long periods of time by "potting" families and are still used successfully in village potteries and art studios. In several respects, the *Parts by Volume* system of compounding new glazes is suggestive of their techniques. This system (PbV) rests on the simple fact that chemical and physical dimensions of glaze materials differ from each other. The humble potters of the Carpathian Mountains knew nothing of the chemical properties of their materials; many decided, at some unknown point in history, to rely on the physical characteristics which they could see, feel, and measure.

The PbV system of glaze-making can definitely be regarded as the most creative approach to glazes. It can be specifically recommended not only for the beginner in public school ceramics programs, but also for serious students and advanced potters who have some understanding of chemical reaction patterns. For the latter this system becomes a rewarding adventure. Its simplicity lends it an overwhelming charm like primitive art, or the force of expressionistic painting. In the beginner, it evokes a true understanding of what a glaze really is—primitive matter in interaction with the raw element of fire. When one's thinking becomes adjusted to the volume-relationships of the PbV system, glaze-making becomes a fascinating task of picking up a cup of this material and a cup of that. And the beauty of it is that it works with amazing results—just what creatively-minded studio-potters need.

A formula and a graph of a very simple low-fire, raw, lead glaze will start us on the adventure of glaze-making by the PbV system. The graph below is very important because it contains the basic concept of the difference between chemical and physical proportions of glaze materials. It can be stated that it enables us to "see" the PbV system in that it essentially visualizes proportions. The formula for the glaze is:

White lead	1 cup	=	300 grams
Local red clay	1/3 cup	=	70 grams
Potters flint	1/2 cup	=	120 grams

The glaze matured to a shiny gloss at cone 04.

On a Parts by Volume scale, as can be observed, more than half the volume-content of the glaze consists of fluxes. The refractory elements in the glaze occupy approximately a third of the amount of the fluxes and silica, and the glass-forming element about a half of the amount of the fluxes. The apparent distortion of the proportions between the flux-alumina-silica ratio, as compared with the same formula when converted into its empirical form, rests on the fact that silica has a very low compound molecular weight. Also, by the addition of clay, which contains twice the amount of silica when compared to alumina, the proportions for the alumina tend to become smaller. When this glaze was converted into an empirical formula, it read:

Fluxes		Alumina		Silica	
PbO	.39	Al_2O_3	.29	SiO_2	2.1

For purposes of comparison, the conversion was only approximate; no chemical analysis of the local clay was made and its

Figure 49. Master potter Steve Andersen with some of his "GNITTIFEPIPS," which are between 29" and 50" high, 1970, University of Colorado.

fluxing-iron and other impurities were not considered. This was not significant for the purpose of the calculation, which was to arrive at a visual pattern. The resulting graph demonstrates the basic differences of both systems.

Therefore, when glazes are compounded on a PbV basis, the following points are important:

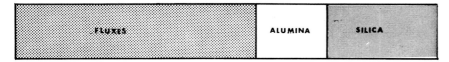

Figure 50. A visual representation of a composition when the physical proper-ties of the chemical compounds are considered. The graphs have been based upon the same glaze. By understanding the difference and proportionate dimension of the empirical and physical properties of glazes, the parts-by-volume system of glaze making is possible.

Figure 51. A visual representation of an empirical composition of a glaze. The graph depicts the relationships of flux-alumina and silicates according to their chemical reaction properties.

1. Fluxes form the large part of the dry glaze.

2. Alumina added in the form of clays should be one 1/4 to one 1/3 of the volume of the fluxes.

3. The silica should make one 1/2 to 3/4's of the amount of the fluxes in the dry glaze batch.

4. When a variety of fluxes are used in a glaze, they should be combined in approximate proportions by the PbW system.

Converted to a percentage basis, the same glaze proportions are:

White lead	61 percent
Local clay	14 percent
Flint	24 percent

Perhaps more important than the development of the original glaze by the "cup" method are, again, the possibilities of adaptation and conversion of this glaze for specific purposes and clay-bodies. The original glaze matured at cone 04 and resulted in a rich, glossy, transparent glaze with a soft light refraction. (Illus-tration 47) When five percent tin oxide was added, a milky light-yellow glaze appeared containing a degree less glossiness. Many original glazes can be developed from such glaze conversions, and the samples below should demonstrate the procedure. The glaze was weighed on a gram scale and the following weights were estab-lished:

Original Glaze:	White lead	300 grams
	Local clay	70 grams
	Flint	120 grams

Figure 52. A simple, low fire, raw leadglaze developed by the cup method and four changes of the original glaze as described in the text.

The glaze translated into gram-concepts (PbW) was easy to change. From experience it was found useful to keep the quantities of the glaze ingredients within certain limits, which are approximately:

Materials	PbV	PbW	Percent
Fluxes	1	100	50-65
Clays	1/4-1/3	25-50	15-40
Flint	1/2-3/4	40-75	35-70

By using this chart, the following glazes were developed from the original glaze and tested. All glazes when fired to cone 04 in a small electric test kiln have proved reliable.

Glaze A.	White lead	240	- flux
	Whiting	60	- flux
	Local clay	70	- alumina & silica
	Flint	120	- silica
Glaze B.	White lead	240	- flux
	Whiting	60	- flux
	Ball clay	70	- alumina & silica
	Flint	120	- silica
Glaze C.	White lead	210	- flux
	Whiting	60	- flux
	Zinc oxide	30	- flux
	Kaolin	70	- alumina & silica
	Flint	120	- silica
Glaze D.	White lead	210	- flux
	Whiting	20	- flux
	Zinc oxide	20	- flux
	Borax	50	- flux
	Kaolin	70	- alumina & silica
	Flint	120	- silica

Notice that the fluxes in each batch always form a whole in this glaze of 300 grams, an amount which was determined by weighing the contents of one cup of white lead of the original glaze.

Figure 53. A group of extruded tubular forms for flower arrangements. Tallest one 18 inches. Cone 8 reduction stoneware by master potter Sheldon Carey, University of Kansas.

In Glaze A, whiting has been substituted for some of the lead and the glaze has lost some of its glossiness. A semi-matte glaze with a beautiful, yellowish tone and a buttery quality resulted: the glaze looked very good on terra-cotta pottery where its yellowish tone turned into a pleasant orange on the red clay. The glaze displayed a very fine grazing pattern when applied in heavier amounts.

In Glaze B, ball clay replaced the local clay and the whiting was retained in the fluxes. As a result of the ball clay, the grazing became more pronounced and visible; the glaze lost its yellowish color for a neutral transparency.

In Glaze C, the addition of zinc oxide and the replacement of ball clay and local clay for kaolin caused the grazing to disappear completely. The glaze displayed a milky opacity and a not-too-brilliant gloss. The glaze was later used over red clay and was found to expose the elevated areas of the clay with good decorative effects.

In Glaze D, four fluxes were combined and an almost perfect, transparent, colorless glaze resulted. The glaze had no grazing, but possessed fine healing properties. By adding seven percent of tin oxide, a fine quality majolica glaze was achieved which responded well to most colorants.

The author hopes that he has amply demonstrated that glaze-making according to the Parts-by-Volume system is possible for every one, and that it can become an exciting adventure when followed beyond the limits of this book. In fact, the student is here urged to explore his own bounds and to use the systems of this study, carrying his experiments into all directions of firing ranges, colors, textures, and materials. Over the years from sources too numerous to recall, the author has collected a number of very simple glazes. These may serve the student as a starting point of beginning some startling explorations in search of the perfect glaze.

Glaze X-l.	White lead	1 cup
	Clay	1/2 cup

Figure 54. A historic picture of the Swedish master potter Wilhelm Kage from Gustafsberg, Sweden, with his student, now Professor Stig Lindberg. Mr. Kages contributions to the development of Scandinavian stoneware concepts are too numerous to mention. His pioneering in technical and aesthetic aspects, his deep research into the original sources of the golden age of ceramics in China, have left a mark on every young potter since.

Figure 55. Stoneware Lions by artist Lisa Larson, Sweden.

Glaze X-2.   Red lead   4 tablespoons
              Whiting   1 tablespoon
              Clay   2 tablespoons

Glaze X-3.   Sodium silicate   8 spoons (waterglass
                                   available in
                                   drug stores)

              Whiting   2 spoons
              Clay   1 spoon

Glaze X-4.   Borax   10 spoons
              Clay   8 spoons

Glaze X-5.   Borax   1/2 cup
              White lead   1 cup
              Clay   1 cup

The glazes were fired to cone 06, 04, and cone 02. Best results appeared at cone 04 where the glazes displayed a slight over firing and some beautiful textures appeared.

Figure 57. Wallplaque, 32 x 26 inches, lowfire glaze cone 05 with reduced lusters at cone 018 in a second firing with photo emulsion picture. Artist-potter Victor Spinski, Delaware.

Figure 56. Round, wheelthrown stoneware forms, cone 9, partially unglazed, by Karin Bjorquist, Sweden.

Figure 58. Master potter Roger Corsaw, University of Oklahoma, among his large glazed pots.

Figure 59. Large, hand-built branch bottle by Nan Bangs McKinnell, wood fired, approximately 30 inches in diameter. Stoneware.

Figure 60. Stoneware, cone 10, photosilkscreen. Victor Spinski, Delaware.

STONEWARE GLAZES

It goes without saying that the systems of changing glazes and compounding new ones will perform just as well when employed for high-fire glazes. Any one of the above glazes could be converted into a high-fire glaze by adjusting the flux-alumina-silica ratio within the batch. Another important factor not to be overlooked is the change of fluxing materials; in high temperature glazes, feldspar, whiting, zinc oxide, dolomite, and ceramic talc become the major fluxes. White lead is not recommended in temperatures over cone 4, since it becomes useless at temperatures beyond cone 6—although small quantities can be used at this cone. *At cones 8 to 9 the ratio between the fluxes and the alumina-silica elements has been found to be nearly half and half.* Again, it should be emphasized that the addition of local fire clays to stoneware glazes is beneficial for the individual qualities that it gives to each piece. The following are two matte glazes which have been tested and found to be very useful. Both have a pleasant opaque quality and good healing properties; they also respond well to coloring substances.

Glaze HX-6.	Cone 8-10	matte
	Potash feldspar	1 cup
	Whiting	1/2 cup
	Ball clay	1 and 1/2 cup
Glaze HX-7.	Cone 8-10	matte
	Potash feldspar	3/4 cup
	Washed ashes	3/4 cup
	Ball clay	1 and 1/2 cup

The above ash glaze is one of the finest ash glazes that this writer has seen. It displays a very smooth, heavily-textured, stony matte that is pleasant to feel. It has a wide firing range, but under cone 8 its textural qualities appear grey. It heals over glazing defects and because of the ash content all colors assume a unifying, subtle grey undertone which is very attractive.

To develop the above glazes, the same procedures as those first

34

described could be followed. The ingredients could be weighed and substituted by other fluxes and clays to form glossy or matte textures according to either of the systems.

BASIC GLAZE CALCULATIONS

At the risk of repetition, the author wishes to point out that *Keramos* has been primarily written to emphasise the more creative approaches to clay and glazes. Nevertheless, facts and reality must be faced, while glaze calculations as such may be of little interest to the beginning artist-potter who is constantly on a hunt for "workable formulas," some exposure to the basics of the system is desirable.

As mentioned at the beginning of the chapter the oxides and compounds used in glaze making are divided into three major groups: the $RO + R_2O - R_2O_3 - RO_2$. The R standing for the *element* itself and the O for oxygen. The RO signifies that the chemical composition of the oxide consists of *one atom of element* and *one atom of oxygen.*

The R_2O indicates two atoms of element and one atom of oxygen.

The R_2O_3 indicates a combination of two atoms of element and three atoms of oxygen.

And the RO_2 means one atom of element and two atoms of oxygen.

It is good to also remember that these are the fluxes (RO), the refractories (R_2O_3), and the glass-makers (RO_2).

THE EMPIRICAL FORMULA AND BATCH WEIGHT RECIPE

In industry and large studios glazes are most often developed using empirical calculations. The formulas resulting are chemically accurate and allow for a uniform repetition of the glaze.

An empirical formula indicates the number of molecules of each participating oxide that is needed to achieve a perfect melting at a given temperature. To be of any practical value the empirical data

has to be converted into measurable quantities. The process is the conversion of the empirical formula into a *glaze batch recipe.* The calculations involved are fairly simple; the requirements of each oxide in the empirical formula are *multiplied* by the number of their molecular, (or, equivalent) weight.

The *molecular weight* of an oxide, or, chemical compound is the total sum of the *atomic weights* of its constituent elements. Some elements appear more than once in their own empirical formula, in such case, the *equivalent weight* of the compound is used in calculations. A basic list of *molecular* and *equivalent* weights useful for calculations follows:

Material		Use for Calculations
Alumina	Al_2O_3	102
Aluminum Hydroxide	$Al_2(OH)_6$	156
Antimony Oxide	Sb_2O_3	198
Barium Carbonate	$BaCO_3$	197
Barium Hydroxide	$Ba(OH)_2$	171
Barium Oxide	BaO	153
Bismuth Oxide	Bi_2O_3	464
Bone Ash	$Ca_3(PO)_2$	103
Boric Acid	$B_2O_3, 3H_2O$	124
Borax	$Na_2O, 2B_2O, 10H_2O$	380
Boric Oxide	B_2O_3	70
Cadmium Sulphite	CdS	144
Calcium Carbonate	$CaCO_3$	100
Calcium Chloride	$CaCl_3$	111
Calcium Oxide	CaO	56
Calcium Phosphate	$Ca_3(PO_4)_2$	103
Cerium Oxide	CeO_2	176
China Clay—Kaolin	$Al_2O_3, 2SiO_2, 2H_2O$	258
Chromium Oxide	Cr_2O_3	152
Chromium Sulphate	$Cr_2(SO_4)_3, 15H_2O$	662
Cobalt Oxide, black	Co_3O_4	241
Cobalt Ox. (cobaltous)	CoO	75
Cobalt Sulphate	$CoSO_4, 7H_2O$	280
Copperas	$FeSO_4, 7H_2O$	278
Copper Carbonate	$CuCO_3$	166
Copper Oxide, green	CuO	80
Copper Oxide, red	Cu_2O	144

Material		Use for Calculations
Copper Sulphate	$CuSO_4$	160
Cornwall Stone	1 RO, 1.16 Al_2O_3, 9 SiO_2	652
Cryolite	3 NaF, AlF_3	420
Dolomite	$CaCO_3$, $MgCO_3$	184
Feldspar, Potash	K_2O, Al_2O_3, 6 SiO_2	556
Feldspar, Soda	Na_2O, Al_2O_3, 6 SiO_2	524
Iron Oxide, red	Fe_2O_3	160
Iron Oxide, black	FeO	72
Iron Sulphate	$FeSO_4$, 7 H_2O	278
Kaolin(ite)	Al_2O_3, 2 SiO_2, 2 H_2O	258
Kaolin, Calcined	Al_2O_3, 2 SiO_2	222
Lead Carbonate (white)	2 $PbCO_3$, $Pb(OH)_2$	258
Lead Oxide	Pb_3O_4	228
Lithium Carbonate	Li_2CO_3	74
Lepidolite	LiF, KF, Al_2O_3, 3 SiO_2	356
Magnesium Carbonate	$MgCO_3$	84
Manganese Carbonate	$MnCO_3$	115
Manganese Dioxide	MnO_2	87
Nickel Oxide, green	NiO	75
Nepheline Syenite	1 RO, 1.5 Al_2O_3, 4.5 SiO_2	447
Potassium Carb. (pearl ash)	K_2CO_3	138
Sodium Carb. (soda ash)	Na_2CO_3	106
Spodumene	Li_2O, Al_2O_3, 4 SiO_2	372
Talc, Ceramic	3 MgO, 4 SiO_2, H_2O	126
Tin Oxide	SnO_2	151
Titanium Dioxide	TiO_2	80
Rutile	TiO_2	80
Zinc Oxide	ZnO	81
Zirconium Oxide	ZnO_2	123

The following form is most widely used for the purpose of converting the empirical requirement into a batch weight:

Material	Empirical Requirement	X	Equivalent Weight	=	Batch Weight
Whiting	0.2	X	100	=	20 grams

When a form as the above is developed with space for all needed compounds the calculating of a glaze becomes a simple task of multiplication, or, if the desire is to convert a batch-recipe into an empirical formula, a task of division.

FROM EMPIRICAL FORMULA TO GLAZE BATCH RECEIPE:

Multiply empirical requirements by the compounds equivalent weight—the result, the batch weight.

FROM BATCH TO EMPIRICAL FORMULA:

Divide the batch weights by the equivalent weights of the compounds to obtain empirical requirements.

To demonstrate the whole process the following, low fire, lead-less, raw glaze has been chosen.

RO	R_2O_3	RO_2
K_2O — 0.2	Al_2O — 0.35	SiO_2 — 2.20
CaO — 0.3	B_2O_3 — 0.2	
ZnO — 0.3		

	The Glaze Batch						Empirical Requirements					
Material	Empirical quantity	X	Equivalent Weight	=	Batch Weight		K_2O 0.2	CaO 0.3	ZnO 0.3	B_2O_3 0.2	Al_2O_3 0.35	SiO_2 2.2
Feldspar, potash	0.2	X	556	=	111 grams		0.2/0.0				0.2/0.15	1.2/1.0
Whiting	0.3	X	100	=	30 "			0.3/0.0				
Zinc oxide	0.3	X	80	=	24 "				0.3/0.0			
Boric acid	0.2	X	124	=	25 "					0.2/0.0		
Kaolin	0.15	X	252	=	38 "						0.15/0.00	0.3/0.7
Flint	0.7	X	60	=	42 "							0.7/0.0

Figure 61. Standard form used by most potters for glaze calculations.

After the omission of minute fractions the test batch turned out to be:

Feldspar, potash	112
Whiting	30
Zinc oxide	24
Boric acid	25
Kaolin	38
Flint	42

Points to remember:

1. Some compounds add more than one oxide to the glaze batch. Most notably the feldspars which add fluxes (potassium, or sodium), alumina and silica. These have to be considered in glaze calculations as demonstrated in the example above. A standard empirical formula for feldspar is $K_2O-Al_2O_3-6SiO_2$ which means that for every molecule of potash, there is also added to the glaze one molecule of alumina, and 6 molecules of silica. Certainly this is an unscientific way to look at the problem, but perhaps an understandable way for the starting student.

   Notice the empirical requirement of feldspar 0.2 also added to the batch 0.2 of alumina and *six times* 0.2 of silica which is 1.2 of the 2.2 required amount.

2. The fluxes in any empirical formula should also form a whole, as demonstrated:

$$
\begin{aligned}
K_2O &- 0.2 \\
CaO &- 0.3 \\
ZnO &- 0.3 \\
B_2O_3 &- 0.2 \\
\hline
\text{total} \quad & 1.0
\end{aligned}
$$

CONVERSION CHARTS

Still another way to save time and effort is to use the following conversion charts in your glaze calculations. Once familiar with the charts they become easy to read, and serve as an *automatic glaze calculator*. Translating an empirical formula into a glaze

Figure 62. Yutaka Kondo, Japan. Traditional forms and beauty are still reflected in the products of Japan's modern master potters. Blue ash glaze vase, the shape is achieved by cutting lines half-way through the wall of the vase and are then pushed out from the inside by the fingers to achieve an effect of opening lips.

batch recipe becomes as easy as reading a road map distance chart. The charts indicate *grams* as the batch weight units, because most glaze experiments in classrooms are carried on a gram basis, but there is no reason, in larger studio situations why these could not be ounces, or, even pounds. To assure success the following steps are recommended:

Step 1. Fill in the empirical requirements of the formula under the symbol of the oxide needed. Using the charts find the batch weight of each *oxide* and insert it under the empirical requirement. (Attention: in case of potash feldspar you are only interested in the amount of *potassium oxide* 0.5.

Step 2. On the left side of the form list the materials intended to be used in the glaze, followed by the batch weight of the compound. (In case of potash feldspar 0.5 is 278.)

Step 3. Carry these numbers across the sheet in their proper columns. This will enable you to see when the empirical requirements have been met. (In case of potash feldspar: The total batch weight is 278, of which 47 are potassium oxide, 51 are alumina oxide and 180 silica. The potassium requirement has been met. Fifty-one parts of alumina have been supplied and 10 more parts are needed, these are supplied by adding 0.1 (empirical) of kaolin, which is 10.2 grams. Now the alumina requirement is met. One hundred ninety-eight parts of silica are needed of which the feldspar supplied 180, and the kaolin 12. This leaves 6 parts to be filled adding flint. 0.1 (empirical) of silica is 6 parts, now the silica requirement is met.

In the above calculation small fractions have been eliminated for ease of calculations. This will in no way affect the outcome of the glaze.

Material		Empirical Requirements				
		K_2O	ZnO	CaO	Al_2O_3	SiO_2
Empirical Requirement		0.5	0.4	0.1	0.55	3.3
Needed Batch Weight		47	32	10	61	198
Feldspar, potash	278	47 / 00			51 / 10	180 / 18
Zinc, oxide	32		32 / 00			
Whiting	10			10 / 00		
Kaolin	10				10 / 00	12 / 6
Flint	6					6 / 0

Figure 63. Form recommended when using conversion charts for automatic glaze calculations.

Conversions of the Most Common Glaze Constituents into Batch Weights

Oxides — RO, R_2O, RO_2

Chem. Compound	Empirical Quantity										
	0.05	0.1	0.2	0.3	0.4	0.5	0.6	0.7	0.8	0.9	1.0
Aluminum Hydroxide	7.8	15.6	31.2	46.8	62.4	78.0	93.6	109.2	124.8	140.4	156
Barium Carbonate	10	20	40	60	80	100	120	140	160	180	200 grams
Bone Ash	5.1	10.3	20.6	30.9	41.2	51.5	61.8	72.1	82.4	92.7	103
Boric Acid	6.2	12.4	24.8	37.2	49.6	62.0	74.4	86.8	99.2	111.6	124
Borax	19.1	38.2	76.4	114.6	152.8	191.1	229.3	267.5	305.7	335.0	380
Whiting	5.0	10.0	20.0	30.0	40.0	50.0	60.0	70.0	80.0	90.0	100
Cornwall Stone	32.7	65.2	130.4	195.6	260.8	326.0	391.2	456.4	521.6	586.8	652
Dolomite	9.2	18.4	36.8	55.2	73.6	92.0	110.4	128.8	147.2	165.6	184
Flint-(Silica)	3	6	12	18	24	30	36	42	48	54	60
Fluorspar	3.7	7.8	15.6	23.4	31.2	39.0	46.8	54.6	62.4	70.2	78
Colemanite and Gerstley Borate	10.3	20.6	41.2	61.6	82.2	102.8	123.4	144.0	164.6	185.2	206
Lead Carb. (Wh. Lead)	12.9	25.8	51.6	77.4	103.2	129.0	154.8	180.6	206.4	232.2	258
Lead Oxide (Red Lead)	11.4	22.8	45.6	68.4	91.2	114.0	136.8	159.6	182.4	207.0	228
Lepidolite	17.8	35.6	71.2	106.8	142.4	178.0	213.6	249.2	284.8	320.4	356
Lithium Carbonate	3.7	7.4	14.8	22.2	29.6	37.0	44.4	51.8	59.2	66.6	74
Magnesium Carbonate	4.2	8.4	16.8	25.2	33.6	42.0	50.4	58.8	67.2	75.6	84

Conversions of the Most Common Glaze Constituents into Batch Weights

Oxides—RO, R_2O, RO_2 (cont.)

					Empirical Quantity						
Chem. Compound	0.05	0.1	0.2	0.3	0.4	0.5	0.6	0.7	0.8	0.9	1.0
Petalite	9.8	19.7	39.4	59.1	78.8	98.5	118.2	137.9	157.6	177.3	197
Potassium Carb. (Pearl Ash)		13.8	27.6	41.4	55.2	69.0	82.8	96.6	110.4	124.2	138
Sodium Bicarbonate	8.4	16.8	33.6	50.4	67.2	84.0	100.8	117.6	134.4	151.2	168
Sodium Carbonate (Soda Ash)		10.6	21.2	31.8	42.4	53.0	63.6	74.6	85.2	95.8	106
Spodumene	18.6	37.2	74.4	111.6	148.8	186.0	223.2	260.4	297.6	334.8	372
Strontium Carbonate	7.4	14.8	29.6	44.4	59.2	74.0	88.8	103.6	118.4	133.2	148
Talc	6.3	12.6	25.2	37.8	50.4	63.0	75.6	88.2	100.8	113.4	126
Zinc Oxide	4.5	8.1	16.2	24.3	32.4	40.5	48.6	56.7	64.8	72.9	81

Clays and Feldspars — R_2O_3

		0.05	0.1	0.2	0.3	0.4	0.5	0.6	0.7	0.8	0.9	1.0
Potash	alumina	5.1	10.2	20.4	30.6	40.8	51.0	61.2	71.4	81.6	91.8	102
Feldspar	silica	18.0	36.0	72.0	108.0	144.0	180.0	216.0	252.0	288.0	324.0	360
	oxide	4.7	9.4	18.8	28.2	37.6	47.0	56.4	65.8	75.2	84.6	94
	total	27.8	55.6	111.2	166.8	222.4	278.0	333.4	389.0	444.6	500.2	556
Soda	alumina	5.1	10.2	20.4	30.6	40.8	51.0	61.2	71.4	81.6	91.8	102
Feldspar	silica	18.0	36.0	72.0	108.0	144.0	180.0	216.0	252.0	288.0	324.0	360
	oxide	3.1	6.2	12.4	18.6	24.8	31.0	37.2	43.4	49.6	55.8	62
	total	26.2	52.4	104.8	157.2	209.6	262.0	314.4	366.8	419.2	471.6	524
Kaolin	alumina	5.1	10.2	20.4	30.6	40.8	51.0	61.2	71.4	81.6	91.8	102 grams
(calcined)	silica	6.0	12.0	24.0	36.0	48.0	60.0	72.0	84.0	96.0	108.0	120
	total	11.1	22.2	44.4	66.6	88.8	111.0	133.2	155.4	177.6	199.8	222
Kaolin	alumina	5.1	10.2	20.4	30.6	40.8	51.0	61.2	71.4	81.6	91.8	102
Ball Clay	silica	6.0	12.0	24.0	36.0	48.0	60.0	72.0	84.0	96.0	108.0	120
	H_2O	1.8	3.6	7.2	10.8	14.4	18.0	21.6	25.2	28.8	32.4	36
	total	12.9	25.8	51.6	77.4	103.2	129.0	154.8	180.6	206.4	232.2	258
Nepheline Syenite		22.4	44.7	89.4	134.1	178.8	223.5	268.2	312.9	357.6	402.3	447
Delmonte Spar		37.3	74.6	149.2	223.8	298.4	373.0	447.6	522.2	596.8	671.4	746

Conversions of the Most Common Glaze Constituents into Batch Weights

Coloring Oxides — Opacifiers

	Empirical Quantity									
Chem. Compound	0.01	0.02	0.03	0.04	0.05	0.06	0.07	0.08	0.09	0.1
Antimony Oxide	2.9	5.8	8.7	11.6	14.5	17.4	20.3	23.2	26.4	29.2
Chromium Oxide	1.5	3.0	4.5	6.0	7.5	9.1	10.6	12.1	13.6	15.2
Cobalt Carbonate	1.2	2.4	3.6	4.8	5.0	6.2	7.4	8.6	8.6	11.9
Cobalt Oxide black	0.8	1.6	2.4	3.2	4.0	4.8	5.6	6.4	7.2	8.0
Copper Carbonate	1.3	2.6	3.9	5.2	6.5	7.8	9.1	10.4	11.0	11.9
Copper Oxide, green	0.8	1.6	2.4	3.2	4.0	4.8	5.6	6.4	7.2	8.0
Iron Oxide, red	1.6	3.2	4.8	6.4	8.0	9.6	11.2	12.8	14.4	16.0
Iron Oxide, black	0.7	1.4	2.1	2.8	3.5	4.2	4.9	5.6	6.3	7.2
Manganese Carbonate	1.1	2.2	3.3	4.4	5.6	6.7	7.8	8.9	10.3	11.5
Manganese Dioxide	0.9	1.8	2.6	3.5	4.4	5.3	6.1	7.0	7.8	8.7
Nickel Oxide, green	0.8	1.5	2.2	3.0	3.8	4.5	5.2	6.0	6.8	7.5
Nickel Oxide, black	0.8	1.6	2.4	3.2	4.0	4.8	5.6	6.4	7.2	8.3
Titanium Dioxide Rutile	0.8	1.6	2.4	3.2	4.0	4.8	5.6	6.4	7.2	8.0
Tin Oxide, stannic	1.5	3.0	4.5	6.0	7.5	9.0	10.5	12.0	13.5	15.1
Zirconium Oxide	1.2	2.4	3.6	4.8	6.0	7.2	8.4	9.6	10.8	12.3
Vanadium Oxide	1.8	3.6	5.4	7.2	9.0	10.8	12.6	14.4	16.4	18.2

COLOR IN GLAZES

In the coloring of glazes, the point must be made that the most desirable colored glazes are produced by intermixing the coloring oxides. These coloring agents are generally used in very small quantities, fractions of percentages—because of their strong coloring properties. Some oxides, if added to a glaze in appreciable quantities, will influence the viscosity of the base glaze. For example, iron oxide (the source of tans, browns, and reds) if added in quantities over five to seven percent will tend to make a glaze more fluid because iron is a strong flux. Fortunately most oxides are used in quantities which do not affect the base glaze. The table which follows indicates the color and limits of the most commonly used coloring oxides. These percentages relate to the amounts of the total glaze batch.

This writer once knew a Swedish potter who had the habit of always throwing a "pinch" of an opposite oxide into the glaze batch before glazing. When he used iron in a glaze, he added a pinch of cobalt and vice versa. This gave most of his glazes a subtle aura, but he was never able to duplicate exactly the tone of a piece if he had a demand for it.

Students should notice that the first chart concerns *coloring oxides* and deals with percentages of the desired oxide in the total weight of the glaze batch. The second chart deals with combinations of oxides sometimes called *raw stains*. These raw stains have to be prepared in advance by the P.b.W. system, and therefore, the chart indicates *parts by weight,* necessary to form the particular stain. Once the stain has been prepared, then it should be used very much like a coloring oxide, in a percentage. One to 5 percent of any stain will give one light, pastel shades of the desired color,

3. Type of glaze (low fire, matte, leadless, etc.)

4. Color

5. Remarks and observations

Example of a test record:

Glaze Test—...#KRX-15   *Cone 04*

low fire, gloss alkaline glaze developed from #KRX-11

transparent

Borax	250
Clay #4	210

Fired in oxidizing temperature the glaze melted well, had a bubbly texture, very transparent. When applied heavier it turned a muddy, yellowish color which was not attractive. No grazing could be observed.

A second firing, with the addition of five (5) percent tin oxide to the mix, did produce some opacity, but the muddy tone remained.

EQUIPMENT FOR TESTING

Illustration 58 shows the equipment which is used in making test batches in a one-man pottery: (1) a used juice mixer or a small hand mixer; (2) several tea strainers with fine mesh screens; (3) an assortment of jars to store samples; (4) a jar of gum tragacanth solution; and (5) the gram scale.

Test batches are prepared as has been described in the section on glaze preparation, and the four vital points followed, with the only difference being one of quantity. When a test batch is being prepared, 100 to 200 grams will usually suffice to cover a number of test tiles. The containers for mixing such quantities should be appropriate in size, and may be fruit jars, jelly glasses, or plastic cups.

Figure 68. Only simple tools are needed to begin meaningful testing of glazes. A scale, jars, paper bags, spoons, tea sieves, most of the items can be found in any ordinary household.

Figure 69. Three types of common test tiles used by studio potters, preliminary testing can be accomplished with flat tiles, but before glazes are actually used on good pots they should be tried on vertical cylinders to observe the effects of flowing.

Figure 70. Leach Pottery, St. Ives, England, 18-inch stoneware with ash glaze containing beach sand. Reduction fired slab construction.

Figure 71. Kurt Ohnsorg, Austria, two earthenware vases with matte glazes. Gmundener Ceramic Seminar, 1967.

TEST TILES

The tiles should be large enough to permit good observation of the fired glaze. Sizes range from three-inch circles to the six- by six-inch tiles found in commercial plants. The real test tile obviously is the first piece put into the kiln and covered with the new glaze. If it were possible, real pieces should be used in all tests, but such experiments would require a large kiln, much time, and many good forms would be destroyed by glaze failures. One solution to this problem is a staggered use of tile beginning with smaller tiles in line—or traxial tests: as glazes are selected for further testing, the size and form of the tiles should increase to allow clearer observation. For best uses, three types of tiles are recommended in this study. Illustration 59 presents the three types: (1) the flat test tile; (2) the vertical tile; and (3) the cylinder which takes the place of a well-formed pot.

Flat test tiles can easily be cut with a drinking glass or cookie cutter from a rolled out slab of clay. The shapes are pressed from the clay, dried, and bisque-fired; larger numbers may then be kept ready for subsequent testing. The vertical test tile comes very close to revealing the properties of a glaze on a real pot, especially when viscosity of a glaze is being tested. They are made by throwing a low cylinder on the potter's wheel, approximately five to six inches high, then slicing the cylinder as one would a pie. Small cylinders will serve well for final tests of selected glazes before the latter are applied to real pots. These cylinders can be coil-built or thrown on the potter's wheel like small cups. When a test glaze is applied to the tile, the tile must be properly marked. The marking should be made with a brush and one of the dark color oxides: a handy marking ink is produced by combining 50 grams of cobalt oxide with one tablespoon of gum solution and adding enough water to achieve a brushing consistency.

For reasons of convenience, the important principles of glaze-testing can be condensed into the following:

1. Select the size of your test batch. Weigh it carefully. A typical size often used is 100 grams. If the PbV system is used, measure your ingredients by *level* spoons.

2. Add water and gum solution, then strain the mix three times; when using the mixer, mix it at least for several minutes.

3. Record all ingredients on the test card.

4. After the firing, observe the glaze carefully for color, texture, grazing, crawling, and any other characteristics which can be described. Enter these on the card. Do not hesitate to use judgments: a very attractive glaze, muddy color, unpleasant texture. These will later help in the selection when further testing is desired.

The first type of test which is helpful to the studio-potter is unrelated to the use of test tiles. As happens in industry, glazes change their appearance when applied to a piece in different thicknesses. Every potter knows that some glazes look very good when applied thickly, while others become ugly and unattractive. The thickness of a glaze on a pot is influenced by two basic factors: (1) the consistency of the glaze slip, and (2) the density of the bisque-fired clay to which it is applied. The second factor can easily be controlled by regulating the temperature in the bisque kiln and by firing the ware at the same cone. The consistency of the slip is controlled in industry by an instrument called a consistometer. The studio-potter, however, can make his own "consistometer" by wrapping five to ten coils of thin electrical copper wire around the eraser end of a pencil; he should then mark the consistency level of his slip on the pencil with a magic marker. Illustration 60 shows a simple pencil-plunger in action. As the water evaporates over a period of several days, the glaze tends to "stiffen-up" and the glaze level will then be under the mark on the pencil. When this occurs, water should be added to the glaze and stirred until the mark is reached. If the pencil shows the glaze above the consistency mark, the glaze contains too much water and more solids must be added. This procedure will allow for a reasonably accurate control of glaze consistency. Generally in tests of small batches, it is recommended that each glaze be tested with a thin application on one tile and a thick application on another.

To assure satisfactory results in studio testing, it is imperative

Figure 72. Swedish artist-potter Karin Bjorquist developing designs for floor tiles.

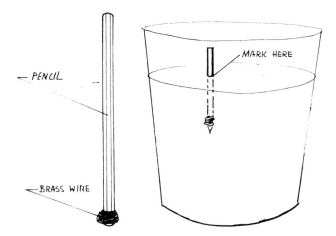

Figure 73. A simple plunger can be made from a pencil with copper wire wrapped around on one end.

Figure 74. Tools and equipment needed to prepare test-batches of glazes. The dry glaze batch is screened three times from container (a) into (b) and back.

Figure 75. Karin Bjornquist, Sweden. Wall and fireplace of glazed tiles.

that the correct type of test or test combinations be selected to serve a given purpose. Being aware of the purpose will aid one in selecting the right test. Some reasons for testing are:

1. To adjust the maturing temperature of a glaze.

2. To adjust common glaze defects such as grazing, crawling, etc.

3. To find new glazes and glaze combinations.

4. To change the texture of glazes without affecting their maturing temperature.

5. To change the color of a glaze: glazes are most attractive when they are either very light or very dark in their color values; the strong middle tones seldom look good on a pot.

The two types of tests most often used in ceramics are the simple line test and the triaxial diagram. Both can be easily understood when applied to a real situation. For purposes of clarity, therefore, the above reasons for testing will be used to introduce the testing procedures.

When changing the maturing temperature of a glaze, a simple line test can be employed on a percentage basis, or on a Parts-by-Weight basis. Depending on the desired increase or decrease in cones, the reader is referred to Rule #1 in glaze changing. Alumina tends to make a glaze matte, but it also contains larger amounts of silica and is, in itself, very refractory. (It also can be used as an additive to raise temperatures.) The test looks like this:

Base glaze	100	100	100	100	100	100	100	100
Additive: flint or clay	-	10	15	20	25	30	35	40
Total dry batch	100	110	115	120	125	130	135	140

If the temperature of a glaze should be lowered, the test could be designed in a reversed order. The practical procedure for actually preparing such a batch is to use small paper bags. To prepare a large batch of the base glaze, dry mix it (three times through a 60-mesh screen *without water*), then divide it into 100 gram portions, each in its own small bag. The next step is to add the amounts of flint or clays desired, marking each bag as it is completed. When this operation is ended, the glazes can be put through the sieve with the water and gum added, and finally applied to the tiles in the usual way.

Line tests are also most useful in adjusting common glaze defects. Grazing, the most common defect, can usually be avoided by the adjustment of fluxes and the replacement of some fluxes by others. To demonstrate this principle, the following test will replace a portion of the lead in a glaze with zinc oxide, a substitution which will prevent grazing of the glaze.

Base glaze:	White lead	300
	Local clay	70
	Flint	120

| White lead | 300 | 280 | 260 | 240 | 220 | 200 |
| Zinc oxide | - | 20 | 40 | 60 | 80 | 100 |

Figure 76. Potter Steve Reynolds from Texas Technological University works on one of his unique sculptures.

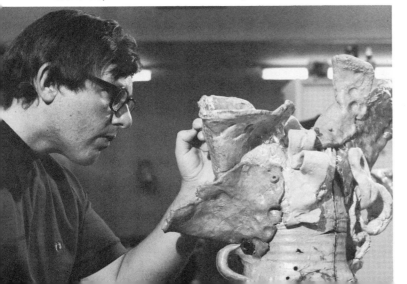

One of the most valuable results of a test is discovering the reaction of a glaze to other chemicals. Some of the most subtle and beautiful glazes have been discovered by the test below, which could be described as a vertical line test:

Base glaze	100	10 percent Feldspar
	100	10 percent Whiting
	100	10 percent Zinc oxide
	100	10 percent Barium carbonate
	100	10 percent Kaolin
	100	10 percent Flint

A promising glaze from such a series could then be submitted to a horizontal line test and the percentages of the particular additive carried out from one percent to its limits in percentages as found in the Table on PbW units.

The second type of test employed extensively in ceramics is the triaxial diagram test which allows the introduction of three components in the test batch and is specifically recommended for the development of new glazes and new color hues. The triaxial diagram test can be designed for a number of situations and sizes. The number of steps along one of the axes determines the extent of the test. Triaxial tests have been designed with as many as 25 steps between the base and the apex of the diagram and with more than 100 test tiles. At the other extreme, the writer has designed small color tests in his studio with four steps between the ends of the diagram. The average number of useful tests between the points on the diagram should not be below five steps (20 percent), but is usually between seven and ten steps.

The triaxial diagram on the following page offers an excellent basis for the study and development of new glazes. At its bases three glazes are used which vary widely in maturing temperatures and composition. Through intermixing these glazes on a percentage basis, new glazes can be developed and the diagram result in gloss, semi-matte, and matte glazes, many of which are very useful.

The diagram approach is also very useful in the development of glaze color combinations. In this case, for example, a reliable glaze is colored with major coloring oxides, iron, red, medium blue, and one batch is left white. The glazes are dry-mixed and for each

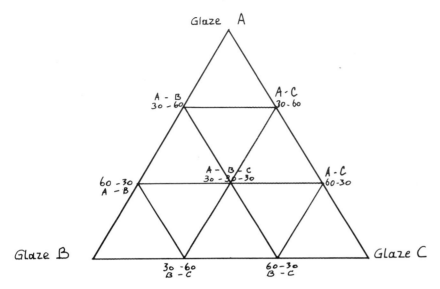

Figure 77. Simple triaxial diagram allowing the intermixture of three different glazes.

Figure 78. A typical majolica base glaze has been colored with 1% cobalt, and 4% iron oxide, one batch is white. The experiment resulted in a number of new hues and values of colored glazes.

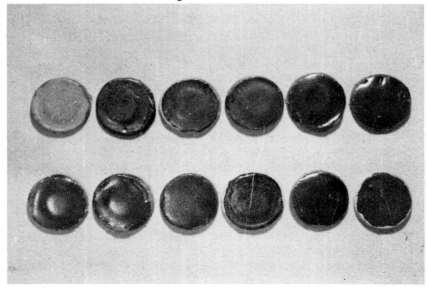

point in the diagram a paper bag is set aside and marked. The mixtures are then weighed and put into the bags on either the PbW or percentage basis, wet-mixed, and fired. The experimenter will be amazed by the richness and beauty of intermixed values and hues which can be achieved from this process. A demonstration of this method can be seen in the graph which follows and in Illustration 64, where iron and cobalt oxides have been used in a typical majolica, white glaze.

Testing, as well as any other ceramic activity, can be exciting: when properly organized it is not greatly time consuming, and the best results follow creative effort. The few simple rules and test patterns which have been described in this chapter will advance the studio-potter toward a good understanding and competent control over his own glazes. These procedures do not diminish the fascination and expectancy which he will inevitably feel when the final test of a glaze is made and the first piece covered with glaze—for the studio-potter, this is the real test.

CHARACTERISTICS OF BASIC GLAZE MATERIALS

WHITE LEAD (LEAD CARBONATE)

1. This remains longer in suspension in the glaze than other lead compounds. It is the preferred form of lead used by studio-potters in raw lead glazes.

2. Its decomposition in the glaze at approximately 800 Fahrenheit causes a violent agitation of the melt which is beneficial and improves final surface qualities of a glaze.

3. It is a very strong flux on temperature ranges from cone 010 to cone 6.

4. It increases the gloss of glazes.

5. It increases the "stretching ability" of the glaze for a better fit on clay-bodies.

6. It decreases the viscosity of a glaze which at times may make a glaze run excessively.

7. It reacts beneficially with most coloring agents.

Figure 79. Small cups used for glaze testing in the author's Silverton pottery.

8. Lead glazes fire best in oxidizing atmosphere.

9. It is poisonous if taken internally. Bernard Leach states that this danger is grossly exaggerated within a studio-potter's perimeter.

10. Vessels covered by lead glazes should not be used for storing acidic liquids.

RED LEAD OXIDE

1. Has no practical advantages for the studio-potter over the carbonate form of lead.

2. It is most widely used in the preparation of lead containing fritts in industry.

3. When used in raw glazes, one percent of bentonite in the slip will aid its suspension.

WHITING (CALCIUM CARBONATE)

1. This remains readily in suspension and is an important component of glazes in all firing ranges.

2. In low-fire glazes, it should be used in smaller quantities, but it becomes a strong flux at higher temperatures.

3. In low-fire glazes it will promote opacity.

4. When added in excess, it will promote matte surface textures through crystallization.

5. It increases the tensil strength of glazes and makes them more resistant to acids.

BORAX

1. Borax can be used to introduce sodiums and boric acid into glazes.

2. It is a major low-fire flux for alkaline glazes.

3. It is highly water-soluble; borax-containing glazes must be ground with a mortar and pestle and used immediately.

4. Generally it brightens glazes. It is also valuable when brilliant hues of blue, blue-greens are desired.

5. Small amounts can be added to glazes on all firing levels to soften their viscosity.

6. An excess of borax in a glaze will cause it to pinhole and blister.

7. It is very often used in combination with lead.

COLEMANITE

1. It is a naturally mined mineral consisting of calcium and boron. It is useful to add boric acid to a glaze in a water-soluble form.

2. It is a popular low-fire flux and renders glazes brilliantly glossy.

3. When added in larger quantities, it promotes mottled effects.

4. It aids the correction of grazing in glazes.

5. It extends the firing range of most glazes by several cones.

DOLOMITE

1. It is a mineral found in nature which contains equal parts of calcium and magnesium. It is used to introduce magnesium into the glaze.

2. It renders to glazes the buttery quality of magnesium glazes, which is considered its greatest asset.

MAGNESIUM CARBONATE

1. It is a very light powder and serves best when used in small quantities.

2. It adds to the development of brilliant glossiness.

3. At lower temperatures it acts as a refractory, but becomes a strong flux above cone 3.

4. Sometimes it promotes opacity in a glaze.

BARIUM CARBONATE

1. It is not as strong a flux as zinc or calcium oxide.

2. At low temperatures it is used to develop matteness in glazes.

3. It lowers the elasticity of glazes and sometimes causes crawling defects.

4. It is very useful in glazes for reduction firing.

ZINC OXIDE

1. Zinc is a powerful flux in the medium and high-fire ranges. In low-fire glazes, it should be used sparingly.

2. In low-fire glazes zinc aids the opacity without impairing their glossiness.

3. It renders glazes viscose.

4. It can be used to correct excessive flow of some glazes.

5. It increases the strength and acid resistance of some glazes.

6. If added excessively, it may result in dry and matte surface textures.

POTASH FELDSPAR

1. It is the most important high-fire flux. It introduces potassium, alumina, and silica into a glaze.

2. In low-fire glazes, used sparingly, it will promote mattes.

3. The compound itself resembles a glaze because of its three components: the alkalies potassium, sodium, and calcium (fluxes), alumina and silica. Feldspar will melt and form a white milky glaze by itself at temperatures over cone 11.

4. It decreases fluidity in a glaze.

5. It increases the mechanical strength of glazes making them more resistant to scratches.

SODIUM FELDSPAR

1. It has many of the attributes of potash feldspar.

2. Compared with potash feldspar, it increases the fluidity of the melt, and decreases the tensil strength and elasticity.

3. In high-fire glazes, it promotes crystallization during prolonged cooling-off periods.

NEPHELINE SYENITE

1. It is a feldspatic material containing more potassium and sodium than feldspar and causing it to fuse at lower temperatures.

2. When substituted for feldspar, it lowers the maturing temperature or increases the fluidity of a glaze.

FLINT

1. Flint is the most commonly used source of silica in glazes.

2. It is the glass-forming component and therefore renders glazes glossy and brilliant.

3. All glazes have to contain a sufficient quantity of silica to form the glassy part of the glaze. In matte glazes the silica content is smaller.

TIN OXIDE (STANNIC OXIDE)

1. It is the most effective of all opacifiers.

2. From five to eight percent will make a glaze completely opaque.

3. When added excessively, a dry and matte surface texture will result.

RUTILE

1. It is an impure form of titanium oxide and contains larger percentages of iron oxide.

2. It promotes opacity, a yellowish tone, and mottled effects in glazes.

CLAYS (KAOLIN, BALL CLAY, AND NATURAL CLAYS)

1. Clays are used to introduce alumina and silica into glazes.

2. Kaolins and ball clays are white firing; they should be preferred in colorless glazes and glazes with brilliant colors.

3. Natural clays will influence color developments because of the larger amount of impurities, mostly in the form of iron, in the clay.

4. Clays act as flotation agents in the glaze slip; they aid in keeping other ingredients in suspension; ball clays are especially effective.

5. Some natural glazes can be easily converted into slip-glazes, and many when fired above cone 8, form a glaze in themselves.

6. The clay content in a glaze strengthens the glaze-coating before it is fired, increasing the handling capability of the piece.

Chapter III

New Concepts in Kilns

Figure 80. Japanese potter feeding coal into the firing chamber.

TYPES OF CERAMIC KILNS

The third element in making pottery is fire. In order to achieve permanence by subjecting his products to intense heat, the potter needs a kiln. Basically, kilns are boxes in which heat can be stored to very high temperatures. They may be extremely simple or extremely complicated. If the "potter" should be a plant employing 400 or more people in the production of ceramic wares, the "kiln" becomes a problem of complex engineering with many control facets to consider. When a kiln has to hold 10 or 20 hand-made pieces in the workshop of an artist-potter, then the design and construction become a problem of individual experimentation.

KERAMOS encourages this approach because the purpose here is not to present a complete, scientific encyclopedia on kiln building, but rather to suggest a human approach which will make individual experimentation meaningful and the end result successful. As with the clay and glazes mentioned in foregoing chapters, most of the valued ceramic art surviving from the past was fired in kilns which would today present a horrible sight to every self-respecting fire marshall in this country: for centuries, however, they have proven safe and functional. This observation is not meant to discourage sensible kiln safety in any way, but merely to stress the fact that safety factors need not deter anyone who wishes to build his own kiln. The intimate relationship to be

Figure 81. A traditional "anagama" kiln preserved at the Kyoto City College of Fine Arts.

Figure 82. A small round kiln, 4 feet inside diameter, fired with four, natural draft, venturi type burners which were discarded by a brick yard, obtained free by the author. The kiln has been built in a shed with removable walls.

gained in such an enterprise is deeply enriching for the artist-potter and the layman. It provides a quicker way to understand the firing processes than can be obtained from manuals and books.

The costs of manufactured kilns are often prohibitive for many potters and schools. Even when using the best materials available, one can usually build a kiln for less than a third of the manufacturer's price for a comparable size. If one cares to cut corners and do without luxuries here and there, the cost can turn out even lower. If well planned, a portable or semi-permanent kiln of medium size can be constructed by anyone interested enough to take the time. In fact, a small stacking kiln can be safely set up within a few hours and fired as soon as the fuel line is connected. Temperatures below 2,000-degrees Fahrenheit are relatively simple to achieve, but those for stoneware depend upon how successfully several factors of the kiln have been balanced. The type of fuel, fuel input, efficiency of the burners, proper kiln design, and damper control all influence the performance of the kiln.

The principles and ideas following later in this chapter have little similarity with the elaborate charts which a ceramic engineer would employ when calculating the design and use of a kiln. If followed, they will aid the kiln-builder to establish that necessary balance between *heat resistance* and *heat radiation* in the practical construction of the kiln. Some of the Oriental kilns were built from old saggars with the thin end forming the inside wall of the kiln containing the intense heat. These early kiln builders perhaps did not understand the theory of what they did, but they certainly worked with one of the most important principles of kiln construction—that *air is the best insulator* we have. In the West we often assume that the heavier a kiln is the better and safer it is. This is not true. Our three-layer brick walls often result in heating fortresses, or another example of our general social philosophy that waste is good for us.

Kilns can be built either outside or inside a workshop. All kilns should have some protection from the elements. Often this takes the form of temporary walls and roofs. In windy regions, small outside kilns will pose firing problems because the wind significantly increases the heat loss through the kiln walls, blows out burners, or causes gas burners to back-fire. When a kiln is built for

Figure 83. Large, round, down draft kilns, 32 feet in diameter. Such kilns are still widely used by brick companies throughout the country.

Figure 84. A medium size, dual-fuel kiln at the Kyoto City College. The kiln uses electricity to reach desired temperatures in faster time and wood, to achieve the effects of flame and reduction.

heavy and extensive reduction firing, heavy smoking results and outside sheds will serve best. Many old potteries in Europe and Asia continue to use primitive-looking sheds with sheet metal roofs and movable walls. During hot summers the walls are completely removed and returned to place when cold weather begins. The author uses this practical solution in the Silverton Mountain Pottery in Colorado. A whole wall of the kiln shed is removable and provides ventilation and safety during the firing.

Building codes and the availability of fuel and building materials will determine the kind of kiln one finally decides upon. While electric kilns limit the potter to moderate temperatures and an oxidizing atmosphere, still they solve many problems. They cause no smoke, and when properly insulated can be placed in any building—including basements. Small experimental gas-burning *stacking* kilns can be *stacked-up* from fire bricks without the use of mortar. It is always best that they be placed outside the shop (salt-glazing and raku kilns belong in this category) because they smoke heavily in order to achieve the best effects, but in doing so develop all sorts of fumes. When not in use, these small kilns can readily be protected from the weather by portable covers made of plastic, canvas, or plywood. The sizes of kilns vary widely from small laboratory test kilns to the huge multi-chambered kilns of the ceramic industry. The *types* of kilns can be limited according to (1) the temperature desired, (2) the fuel used, and (3) the construction of the kiln. Within the scope of this book an artist-potter or a school would probably identify their needs from among the following types:

1. Temperature: Low-fire   below 2,000° F.
                   High-fire   above 2,000° F.

2. Type of fuel: Electricity
                    Natural gas
                    Bottled gas
                    Wood
                    Coal
                    Oil
                    Combination of fuels.

Figure 85. Potters Tom Collins, Bill Farrell, and student Brad Kato checking a draw trial of the salt kiln behind them.

3. Construction: Up-draft
                Down-draft
                Single-chamber
                Multi-chamber

An interesting new concept in kiln construction is that of equipping the kiln with dual or combination fuel systems. The idea probably originated in Japan where such kilns are now used in educational institutions. Students of ceramics at the City College of Fine Arts in Kyoto are successfully using a kiln which burns both electricity and wood. The firing chamber of the kiln is built into a square box containing heating coils imbedded in the sides and a fire-box is attached at the front. The flue outlet is placed in the middle at the bottom of the back of the kiln. Professor Kondo of the City College of Fine Arts has described the success of the solution. The kiln allows a much better control of the temperature raise (which is supplied by electricity) while reduction and the natural effects of flame are still available. It also cuts down drastically on the amount of wood which would be required for a normal wood firing.

Very little experimentation with dual fuel systems has been carried on in the West. The author has developed a *gas-oil* fuel system, however, which he successfully uses in Silverton. The success of an oil-burning kiln depends upon the vaporization of the oil, which in turn allows for a more complete combustion and thus a hot, smokeless flame. In Silverton, a system was designed in which a thin cast-iron plate is pre-heated to red heat by a set of home-made, low-pressure, bottled gas burners. When the plates are sufficiently hot, the oil is turned on and allowed to drip slowly onto the hot plates. The oil instantly vaporizes into tiny droplets and is ignited by the heat. The firing requires much time and effort as the burners can never be left unattended. They must constantly be adjusted for gas and oil flow because each affects the other. It took more than 18 hours to reach a cone 9 temperature in a well-insulated 14 cubic-foot kiln. Despite the results achieved, the author feels that there is much room for experimentation whereby systems with desirable criteria could be combined to achieve better control and better results in firings.

Electric kilns are now manufactured in many sizes for reasonable prices. Many are equipped with Kanthal A-1 heating elements and attain temperatures up to 2,300° Fahrenheit. These high-fire electric kilns, which allow firing up to cone 8, have made public school programs in ceramics possible and popular. Most manufactured kilns serve well for many years, and when the elements burn out they can be replaced. In addition, since electric kilns require no chimney, they are easier to build. Notwithstanding their advantages, however, they provide less of a challenge to the artist-potter because his opportunity to fire and control the kiln is limited to a simple turning on and off of switches. Electric kilns, at least as they are now manufactured in the United States, are not recommended for reduction firing. Many of the challenging glazes which today's potters desire most require the effects that carbon and gases of other fuels produce.

In fuel firing kilns glazes appear to mellow, many variations in color and tone occur depending on the flame and draft patterns in the kiln chamber, and notably with iron and copper oxides, the oxygen ratio in the kiln affects the color. Celadon and Copper Red glazes develop only when fired to maturity in a reducing (carbon-rich) atmosphere. Carbon has a great afinity for oxygen at high temperatures and will absorb it from the iron, or copper in the glaze. When through this process of reduction either iron, or copper become deprived of their oxygen, they remain suspended in the glaze layer as particles of pure coloidal metal. Copper becomes a beautiful red with occasional blue or purple areas, and iron turns into a green.

In Europe and the Orient many kilns are still either wood or coal-burning. Some are elaborate multi-chambered tunnel kilns such as the European elliptical tunnel kilns used in brick and tile manufacturing, or the Oriental climbing kilns. Most of them are now fired with hard anthracite coal which is stoked into the kilns through strategically located fire boxes and stoke holes. The disadvantage for a Western potter to rely upon a wood or coal-burning kiln lies in several factors: the expense and availability of fuel, the storage of fuel, the constant attention the kiln needs during firing, and the excessive smoking such a kiln develops, particularly during the early stages of firing. If one can afford this type of kiln for experimental reasons, it will provide excitement during the process of firing that is quite a thrill. Experience and a lot of patience are required to fire a wood-burning kiln successfully. Perhaps one of the best known wood-burning kilns in the West is the Leach, a three-chambered climbing kiln located in St. Ives, England. Mr. Leach built this kiln after a model encompassing some of its famous Oriental predecessors. For fuel it uses completely dry pine logs five to six inches thick and some two and a half feet long. The kiln fires to stoneware temperatures in 30 hours. The stoking of the kiln is done by experienced "stokers." In contrast, near Seto, Japan, there is a coal-burning kiln at the

59

Figure 86. A close-up of an experimental gas-oil, dual-fuel system. The fire is started with butane gas through conventional, home built burners constructed from standard pipe fittings. The oil-line enters the firing chamber from above, once the metal plate inside the fire chamber is red hot from the gas flame the oil is turned on dripping onto the plate, vaporizing immediately from the heat.

Figure 87. Ottani pottery in Japan with a "noborigama" (climbing) kiln in the background. Climbing kilns are usually built into a natural slope.

Tamiji pottery used by the Kato family in the manufacture of rice bowls. A normal load in this kiln consists of 24,000 rice bowls and is fired to cone 10, also in 30 hours. Such a comparatively short firing cycle is called a "fast" fire. From the twentieth hour on, the kiln is heavily reduced—a process which involves stoking the four fire boxes every three minutes. Any oxidation toward the end of the firing would cause the porcelain to become eggshell or greyish. Much depends upon a successful firing. It is conceivable that smaller kilns could be built for firing cycles of 10 hours.

Perhaps oil-burning kilns are next in difficulty to be fired. Although easier to handle than wood burners, they still pose problems which should be considered. Oil burners may be a valid solution where gas is not available, or where intense reduction is called for. They have an advantage over wood-burning kilns in that they are easier to control. Also oil is more readily stored than wood, which always requires large storage space. At the same time, effective oil burning necessitates the use of elaborate injection-type forced-air burners with blower attachments. These are expensive and often prove impractical because of limited space around the kiln. A number of *natural draft* oil-burning systems do exist, and some have been successfully utilized by artist-potters. Nevertheless, they all are difficult to start and to control during the firing. To fire such a kiln successfully takes experience and a lot of honest perspiration. Essentially, the successful use of oil for fuel to reach higher temperatures depends upon efficient vaporization of the oil before ignition: in forced-air burners this is accomplished by the pressure of the air, in home-made drip-burners by the heat of the base plate. With smaller well-insulated kilns up to six cubic feet capacity, when extremely high temperatures are not needed, *weed burners* functioning on light oil or kerosene can be used. These are available in any farm supply store. They burn with a clear blue smokeless flame of approximately 2,000° Fahrenheit. For *raku* kilns they are ideal because of unavoidable reduction during the firing process.

Perhaps the kilns most popular with the studio-potter, colleges, and many high schools are gas kilns. Both *natural* and *bottled* gas can be used and are economical, being second in economy only to electric kilns. While they do require a chimney or other type of

Figure 88. View inside the shed showing a Kyogama style noborigama kiln.

"Hud" on top of the kiln, they at the same time eliminate the need for elaborate fire boxes, fire holes, and expensive burners. They are also easier to control and to avoid the hazards of excessive smoking. Reduction is relatively easy to accomplish by a simple change of the oxygen-gas ratio, which usually involves only a slight readjustment of the valve. To a large extent gas kilns have all the advantages of direct flame firing which the wood, coal, and oil kilns provide and only a few of their disadvantages. The efficiency of the kiln depends upon the flow of gases through the chamber. The most effective speed for kiln gases is between three to five feet per second. Gas burners are less expensive and are available in many capacities for low or high pressure. Burners are relatively easy to build from standard pipe fittings, and therefore usually trim significantly the overall cost of the kiln. The kiln walls are not exposed to hard-hitting (or so-called "dirty") flames, thus eliminating the need for heavy linings in the kiln. Where *natural gas* is available it should be preferred, but this does not by any means exclude *bottled* gas. In Silverton, an 18 cubic foot kiln built from heavy fire brick is fired by three forced-air, portable *torch-burners* which are fed from a 500 gallon, LP gas tank. The kiln fires to cone 11, with medium reduction (which at intervals is increased by oil injection through the fire holes) in seven hours. It uses approximately 35 gallons of gas at a price of 15 cents per gallon. The total cost of a glost firing is $4.25. The kiln usually is staked with $250 to $350 worth of art wares. Because of its medium size and quadrangular design, the kiln contains almost no cold spots and very few pieces are throw-aways. This particular kiln can readily be fired three times each week. Much cracking of wares has been eliminated by setting the kiln the evening before the actual firing, heating the kiln to 200° Fahrenheit, and leaving the pots in this heat over-night. This type of preheating is especially recommended when firing single-fire glazes. Gas-fired kilns allow the shop work in a one-man pottery to go on almost undisturbed. If not too large, they can be built safely in a corner of the studio. They eliminate the need and dangers of excessive fire boxes.

The following ideas and principles of kiln-building are presented with the needs of the artist-potter and the artist-teacher in mind. Because of the need and goals of small-scale potteries and schools, gas kilns will necessarily receive the most space. This writer has not yet met a studio-potter who did not wish to experiment with the building of an ideal "reduction" kiln. A courageous but meaningful beginning coupled with an experimental attitude can turn out to be very rewarding. The building of one's kiln will contribute to the excitement that the use of fire lends to the making of pottery.

IDEAS AND PRINCIPLES IN KILN-BUILDING

The efficiency of any kiln depends upon three factors which have to be brought into a working balance: (1) *heat resistance* of the kiln materials which determine how high a temperature a kiln can withstand, (2) *heat radiation,* and (3) the *construction* of the kiln. In proper balance these three factors will allow the accumulation

Figure 89. Brother of Kenji Kato, checking temperature of large kiln, firing 24,000 porcelain rice bowls to cone 10, using coal for fuel. His wife carrying their younger son is looking on, the kiln has been firing all day and night and the morning sun can be seen behind the kiln.

of heat to the desired level. Periodical ceramic kilns are designed to reach a certain heat level, and under normal circumstances are then turned off to cool slowly. The normal cool-off of a kiln should take two to three times as long as the actual firing. To-

Figure 90. Kato's own studio kiln in which he works evenings and Sundays. The kiln is oil fired with one oil burner visible in the picture, the kiln fires to cone 11.

Figure 91. Paul Soldner, Aspen, Colorado, tending a small, stacked *raku* kiln during a demonstration in Texas.

gether, the firing-up and the cool-off are called a *firing cycle*. The following statements have been collected to aid the potter in the actual building of his kiln, and to assist him in the achievement of the *resistance-radiation-construction* balance. Many of the statements are based upon complex scientific findings, but they have been condensed into readily understandable concepts.

A very common error in home-built kilns is the neglect of proper bottom insulation, which results in unnecessary heat loss. The thickness of the kiln bottom should always correspond to the thickness of the walls.

Small and medium size kilns do not need a concrete foundation, for bricks can be laid directly upon a layer of fine builders' sand.

Concrete foundations for large kilns should in all directions always be at least a third larger than the kiln proper. They should be anchored below the frost line when the kiln is constructed outside.

Kiln dimensions are best planned around the measurements of available kiln shelves and the dimensions of the bricks. Patterns of kiln shelves can be laid out on the floor and the kiln planned around them with the brick size in mind. This will eliminate any waste of kiln space and materials.

When planning a kiln around "shelf sizes," ample space should be left between the shelves in order to allow for a proper circulation of the heat throughout the kiln.

The use of *frames*, or *"skeletons,"* of angle iron are always recommended in the building of a kiln. They will generally strengthen the whole structure and prevent kilns from coming apart. Such frames should be constructed before the actual building begins and the bricks then laid *into the frame*. This procedure will avoid slanted walls and uneven corners.

Kilns can be built from many materials extending all the way from mud mixed with straw to the most sophisticated *insulation fire bricks*. From experience, the author considers it wise to use the best material available. There are mixed opinions among potters in this country as to which is better, insulating or heavy-fire bricks. In constructing a studio kiln, the selection is usually determined by the type and purpose of the kiln. Costs are not as important as some would like to believe. Availability of particular materials is another matter, often making the one at hand the best.

Enclosed air is the best insulator available. Since insulation affects the efficiency of a kiln, all kilns have to have some form of insulation. One of the principles of heat radiation is to achieve a given temperature in the middle of the kiln chamber, which means that the whole kiln must be heated to a corresponding temperature—which depends upon the insulation factors of the materials and the distance of the materials from the heat source. In simplest terms, this is why the fire box is the hottest place in the kiln. In principle, this means the less materials by weight one uses in the construction, that much less one has to heat up later.

Insulating fire bricks, when available, are best to use in kiln building. They can be readily worked into any shape with woodworking tools, which is a factor especially helpful in the construction of arches. They are not, however, recommended for use in fire boxes of large kilns, or at any place in the kiln where they are directly exposed to hot flames. Such ports or boxes should be lined with *heavy* fire bricks. They also have one drawback: when roughly handled, they break easily.

Heavy fire bricks, also called standard fire bricks, have less insulating capacity but are readily available from almost any building supply dealer in the country. They will withstand much more handling before they break, but pose a problem when they have to be "cut" into special shapes.

Castables and other insulators, there exist numerous new products on the market which may be of interest to potters building a kiln. The wide variety does not allow to catalog them here, but printed materials concerning each are readily available from the manufacturers. Castables can be used for arches, kiln floors, and fire holes, some stand temperatures of up to 3,200°F, and are easily mixed in a wheelbarrow. Among the most popular insulating materials which can save on bricks and effort are the "blanket" type materials, Kaowool one of them. More about those is presented later in this chapter.

Saggar-blocks can be used by the potter for smaller, experimental kilns. They are made from slabs in the form of "large cigar

Figure 92. Professor Bill Farrell and students at the Chicago Art Institute during the construction of a salt kiln. The bricks are stacked without mortar.

Figure 93. Rice bowls placed in saggers are being stacked into a large coal fired kiln at the Tajimi pottery in Japan.

63

Figure 94. Large flower pots are stacked inside each other. Wads of fire clay is being used to support the pots in their position.

boxes" from a mixture of 50 percent fire-clay and 50 percent grog, and fired in a standard kiln.

Some *heat loss* will always occur through the kiln walls. This can be reduced efficiently by using insulating materials. In large kilns with long outdrawn firing cycles, this heat loss can be formidable as the heat has time to soak through the walls. This *soaking factor* is of no practical significance in smaller periodical kilns because the short firing cycle is too short for any abnormal soaking.

In the planning of a kiln with a firing chamber of less than *six cubic feet*, *four-and-a-half inch* to *six-inch* walls are sufficient. Kilns as large as *six cubic feet* to *18 cubic feet* should have walls at least *nine inches* thick. Kilns above *18 cubic feet* of firing space may require *12 to 16 inches* of wall thickness, depending upon the type of kiln and the firing temperatures desired.

In kilns with a firing duration of 12 to 14 hours, it is possible to use the less expensive heavy bricks because the soaking factor is not important. In larger kilns some form of effective insulation is almost always necessary. Wall thickness should be based upon brick thickness.

Figure 95. Commercial kilns at a typical college pottery lab. At left a 30 cubic foot Alpine, up-draft kiln, and at the right a Denver Fire Clay Co. Muffle kiln. Both kilns can be fired to cone 10.

When actually building a gas kiln, one should keep in mind the flow of gases. Abrupt corners will impede the flow and cut down on the efficiency of the kiln. Such corners can be filled out with specially fitted bricks, or fire-clay forms. A good mixture to make such forms can be made from 80 percent fine grog, and 20 percent fire-clay. This mixture will not shrink excessively and will hold its shape.

Ceilings and door openings larger than 24 x 24 inches should be constructed from arches: for smaller kilns a *corbel-arch* will suffice.

Often a significant heat loss occurs through the top of kilns. This can be avoided by an extra layer of loose insulation. Vermiculite, a good insulator available from lumber yards, will not burn. To use it effectively one should cover the kiln with two layers of household heavy-duty aluminum foil and then pour the vermiculite on top of the foil cover. This will prevent the finer particles of the loose material from falling into the kiln through cracks during the firing. The foil should be placed on top of the kiln glossy side down: in this way the reflective property of the aluminum will *throw* the heat back and thus form another layer of insulation.

Searset and Laytite are two brand names for commercially available *high fire mortars.* They will withstand temperatures of up to 3,000° Fahrenheit and are best used in the form of a slip. The bricks are dipped and laid very tightly with as little mortar joint as possible.

High-fire mortars can be made from a mixture of 50 percent fire-clay and 50 percent fine grog. If preferred, the grog can be replaced with very fine builders' sand. These mortars will not "stick" permanently, as do the commercially purchased materials, but for more permanence up to 30 percent feldspar can be added.

Smaller *stacking kilns* can be constructed without the use of mortar. This type of construction requires fairly square bricks and a frame to keep the kiln safely together during the firing.

The *floors* of kilns should always be constructed from heavy fire brick. They must stand more physical abuse than the walls.

In *up-draft* kilns, floors should be *lifted* to allow the flames to spread under the floor to achieve a better distribution of the heat.

Figure 96. Master potter Paul Soldner demonstrates the use of exelsior in the reduction of *raku* fired pots.

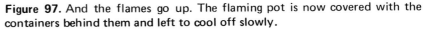

Figure 97. And the flames go up. The flaming pot is now covered with the containers behind them and left to cool off slowly.

Figure 98. Potter Jim Cantrell from Bereta, Kentucky, examines a vessel just being taken out of the kiln.

Figure 99. Among the new "space-age" materials Kaowool, manufactured by Babcock & Wilcox Refractories, lends itself well to build a "paper-hangers kiln." The material comes 24 inch wide, and the pieces were "hung" over a corrugated cardboard form. Thinned out highfire, self-setting mortar was used to keep the pieces together.

Figure 100. As this kiln is experimental, enough fire holes were left open on all sides to experiment with different burner systems. The fire chambers and floor of the kiln were built from conventional refractories. The kiln was built as a research project, by the author, sponsored by Babcock & Wilcox Refractories Division.

In *down-draft* kilns the floor should be planned on the same level as the burners, because this aids the flow of gases through the kiln and avoids unnecessary heat loss through the draft channels.

The most efficient design for a kiln is *square*. The closer the basic form resembles a cube in its dimensions the better the kiln will function. Tall firing chambers are difficult to fire and often contain cold spots which result in many throw-aways.

Flue channels leading to the chimney underneath the floor of a down-draft kiln should be as large as the *setting space*. Their depth should be approximately 15 percent of the height of the kiln chamber.

To aid the flow of gases and create a good draft, the *tunnel*, or opening between the kiln and the chimney, should create a "bottle neck." The size should be somewhat larger than the chimney diameter on the kiln side and *taper* into the chimney.

Chimneys function better when they taper at the top. The lower part of a chimney should always be built from heavy fire bricks.

Chimneys should always be built as close to the kiln as possible. If they are removed from the kiln, an additional foot of height should be added for every two feet of horizontal draft.

It is better to build a chimney too large and regulate the draft with a damper than to build it too small. One of the most common causes for inefficient gas kilns is an inefficient chimney.

The *chimney diameter* will vary with the fuel used. Wood, coal, and oil-burning kilns generally need larger chimneys. When forced air burners are used on a gas kiln, the role of the chimney becomes somewhat less significant. Recommended dimensions for chimney diameters are: wood, coal, and oil-burning kilns 15 percent to 25 percent of the kiln floor area. Gas-fired kilns will function effectively with a chimney diameter of 10 percent to 15 percent of floor space.

The common practice for *chimney height* is to allow *three feet* of chimney for every foot of down-draft.

Up-draft kilns function as their own chimney. They do require larger *hoods* of metal when constructed inside to collect the heat ensuing from the kiln and conduct it safely through the ceiling.

Chimneys can also be constructed from two sheet-metal pipes. For example, putting an eight-inch pipe into a 12-inch pipe and packing moist fire-clay between the two pipes will result in a tight and sturdy chimney of a desired height.

Dampers can be made from discarded kiln shelves. For small kilns "splits" can be used. Splits are fire bricks of half the normal thickness. A damper should be placed between the kiln and the chimney, or the lower part of the chimney.

Wood and coal-burning kilns need sufficiently large *fire boxes.* To reach stoneware temperatures, one square foot of fire box should be allowed for every five square feet of kiln floor. To facilitate the best possible combustion, they should provide space for ashes and an ample oxygen supply.

The success of any kiln is connected closely with the input and heat-storing capacity. If a kiln for the first time performs poorly, more input (another burner, more gas pressure, or an auxiliary fire box) may be added. Often another layer of insulation may solve the problem. In such a case it is doubly important to have the added insurance of ample chimney size when more input of fuel should prove necessary.

All periodical kilns will expand and crack during firing and will settle back after cooling. Framework on kilns prevents them from falling apart.

THE BURNERS

Burners as kilns are basically simple when designed for low-pressure and natural-draft kilns. They become more complex,

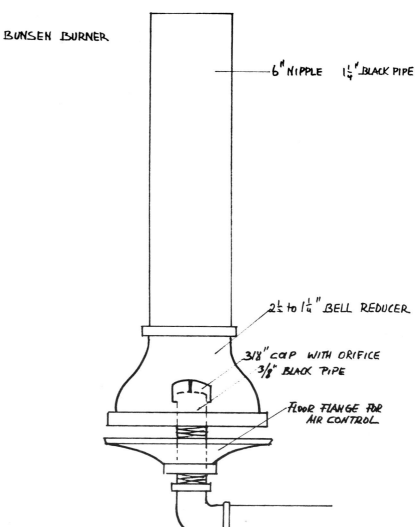

Figure 102. A simple, BUNSEN-BURNER constructed of standard pipe fittings, in sets of two, four, six, or eight it can heat a sizable kiln to stoneware temperatures.

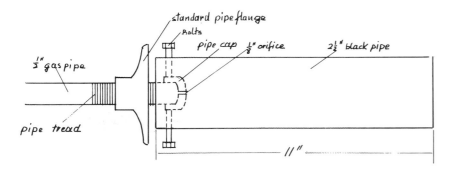

Figure 101. A burner constructed from standard pipe fittings. This burner has been used to fire kilns up to 27 cubic feet capacity to cone 9 and 10. Sets of six such burners were used for the larger kiln. A single burner will serve well for raku firing.

however, where fuels have to be atomized under pressure and forced draft becomes necessary. Some gas burners and oil burners need elaborate fan and orifice arrangements which do not lend themselves well in home construction or experimentation. The ideas set forth here are of simple burners which have been used and proven reliable in a variety of kilns.

A simple and effective burner for oil fuels are weed-burners which are available in hardware stores. They use light oil or kerosene and produce a smokeless hot flame of over 2,000° Fahrenheit. A set of four will easily heat a medium-sized kiln.

Simple natural-draft gas burners can be built from standard pipe fittings and nipples. The investment in a pipe-cutting tool, a tread-cutting tool, and two pipe wrenches is well worth it. Some simple rules need to be followed: (1) use pipe putty on all connections to avoid the escape of gases; (2) try out any burner design before

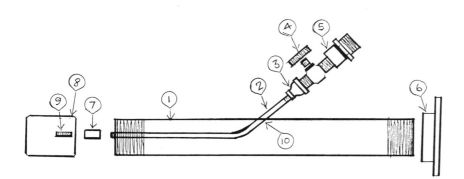

Figure 103. The Soldner oil burner. The burner fires best with kerosene. Forced air can be obtained with a simple vacuum cleaner suction fan connected to the burner in reverse. Used with commercial type pressure fans any size of kiln can be successfully fired with this burner.
(1) 1 1/2" black iron nipple 12" long, (2) 1/8" black iron nipple 8" long, (3) 1/8" to 3/8" reducer (bell), (4) regulator valve, all brass with two ends 3/8" male fittings, (5) hose coupling, male end and 3/8" female on valve end, (6) 1 1/4" black iron floor flange (as adapter to fan unit), (7) 1/8" coupling (to facilitate extension of burner length), (8) 1 1/2" coupling (to facilitate extension of burner length, (9) 1/8" close nipple to adjust length of oil supply to appropriate setting, (10) drilled hole and welded to join pipes. The total cost of the Soldner burner is under $5.00.

making a set of burners; and (3) use all necessary precaution when working with flammable fuels.

THE PIT KILN

It is easy to imagine that the earliest forms of kilns were small tunnels dug into the banks of rivers, close to where clay was readily at hand. It is amazing to note the persistence of artist-potters (once they achieved a certain level of knowledge) in seeking harmony or completeness in their craft by building their own kilns. Perhaps some far removed desire, a primitive urge to do the whole process, or just a yearning for wonder, is what motivates the artist-potter in his search for an ideal kiln.

A pit kiln can be extremely simple, effective, primitive, and often inexpensive. It satisfies much of the yearning to search and experiment with kilns. Pit kilns may be sunken entirely into the ground, or they may be *half dug-out* as in the case of the Japanese *anagama* kilns. Anagamas are traditional Japanese multi-chambered kilns in which half of each chamber lies below the ground level. These kilns are often built from fire bricks and the part protruding above the ground is additionally insulated with a mixture of clay, straw, and ashes. They are held together by wooden beams on the outside which also serve as the main supports for the sheet metal roof. Such a kiln is being actively used by students at the City College of Fine Arts in Kyoto.

Pit kilns have a variety of uses: wood firing, salt glazing, raku, and ordinary bisque and glost firing. They can be built for wood, oil, and gas firing. Because of their placement in the ground, they have an extra added safety appeal.

The kiln presented in the drawing has been selected because of its adaptability to any fuel system. As with other pit-kilns the potter has a choice of either sinking the kiln entirely into the ground or of leaving a part of it above ground level.

Single chambered pit-kilns are essentially short tunnels and will heat up faster in the front close to the fire box. To avoid over-firing of the pots, saggars can be used when necessary. Large pots make good saggars. They can be thrown or slab built from a mixture of half and half of fire-clay and grog, and pre-fired in the same kiln.

THE ELECTRIC KILN

Electric kilns are easily available from many manufacturers in the United States. Their costs vary with the size of the kiln, the firing capacity, and the accessories included. Wherever it is possible to purchase such a kiln, it is recommended because the savings made by a potter in building his own electric kiln are not enough to justify the effort. Perhaps the real value of building an electric kiln is an educational one. Most electric kilns are portable and built into prefabricated boxes. They have no need for chimneys, fire holes, or fire boxes and can be placed inside classrooms and studios. The wiring of electrical kilns is relatively simple, and wiring charts of resistance wires and elements along with recommendations are usually supplied by the manufacturers.

In attempting to build an electric kiln, one should observe the principles regarding foundations, frame, wall thickness, arches, and top of kiln just as much as for other types of kilns. To aid one to construct such a kiln, the following additional information may be useful.

For kilns which are to be used under 2,000° Fahrenheit, any *nichrome* elements will perform well. These are available from appliance repair shops and can be purchased by the foot. The shops usually have charts which indicate the necessary data regarding KW-input and wiring.

For kilns above this temperature, Kanthal A-1 wires are available. These will stand temperatures up to 2,370° Fahrenheit. They can often be purchased in ready-made resistance coils from suppliers of ceramic kilns. They are sold as *replacement* elements.

The normal input for a kiln expected to reach stoneware temperatures with proper insulation is approximately 5 KW (Kilowatt) for every one cubic foot of kiln space. Manufactureres for such resistance wires recommend the following scale of input for a variety of kilns. The insulation should not be under six inches of insulating fire brick.

In principle, one should use as heavy a wire gauge as possible. In high temperature kilns the gauge of the wire will influence the life of the coils. The elements should be supported along their whole length, and the grooves holding the coils should have a larger diameter than the coils themselves.

For operation of the kiln above 2,000° Fahrenheit, the best coil diameter is five to six times the diameter of the wire.

Figure 104. Potter Don Reitz tending a raku kiln constructed from a large trashcan, notice the burner and how far it is from the burner port. Small kilns often pose the problem of too much burner input, one way to solve this problem is to leave the burner further out from the port.

SIZE OF KILN	INPUT IN KW
300 cubic inches	1.6
500 cubic inches	2.5
1 cubic foot	5.0
2 cubic feet	7.5
3 cubic feet	9.0
4 cubic feet	11.0
5 cubic feet	14.0
10 cubic feet	22.0

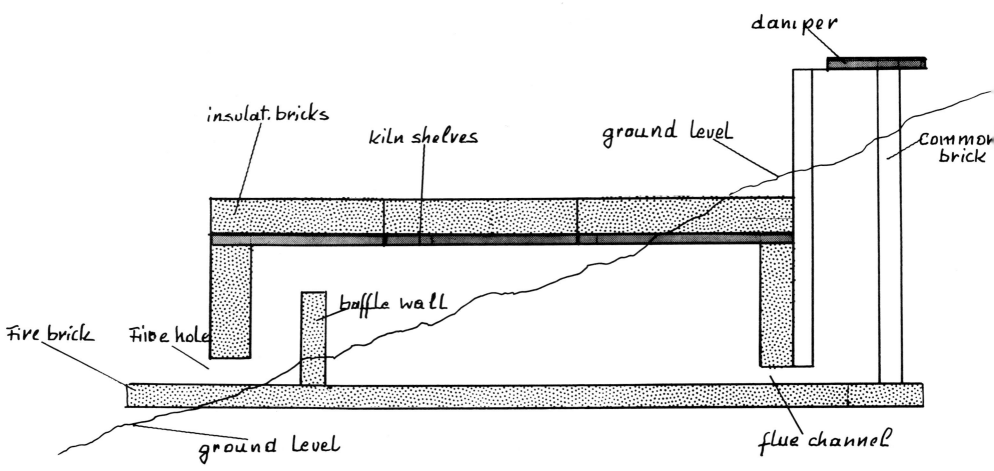

Figure 105. A practical and thoroughly safe *PIT KILN,* the kiln has many advantages for schools and small studios in that it eliminates the need of shelves and elaborate frame work. The fact that it is partially submerged lends it extraordinary safety.

KILN DESIGNS

WALL DETAIL:
1. COMMON BRICK
2. 1" LAYER OF KAO-WOOL
3. 2¼" LAYER OF INSULATIN FIRE BRICK

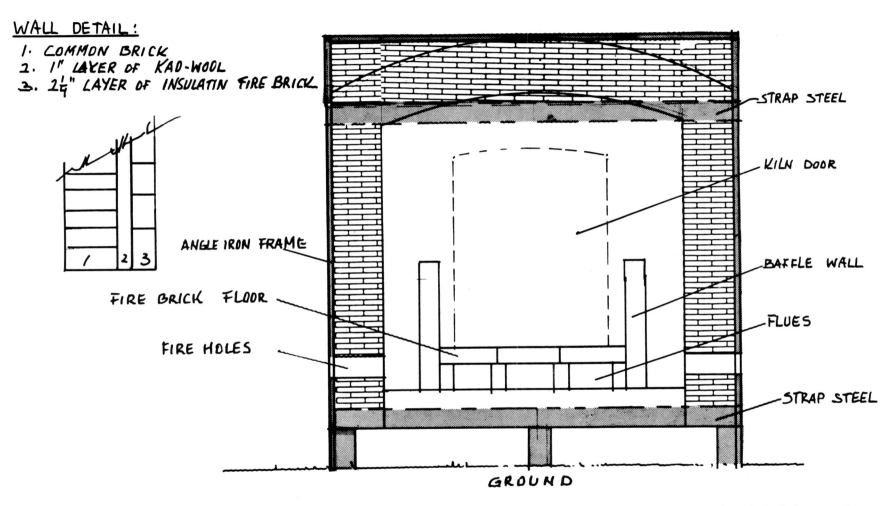

STRAP STEEL

KILN DOOR

BAFFLE WALL

FLUES

STRAP STEEL

ANGLE IRON FRAME

FIRE BRICK FLOOR

FIRE HOLES

GROUND

Figure 106. This is a basic, well-proportioned design of a roman-arch kiln which has been thoroughly tested over many years and can be built in many sizes. When the kiln principles as presented before are followed an extraordinary economical kiln is the result. The wall detail shows a new "space-age" material KAOWOOL manufactured and sold by Babcock & Wilcox Refractories Division. It is inexpensive and a highly effective, easily used insulator. It comes in blanket form and is therefore readily handled. The kiln is lined with insulating fire bricks for necessary strength, then the Kaowool insulation and has an outer shell of common red brick.

Figure 107. Stacked kiln built as a graduate assignment by Less Lawrence, University of Arizona.

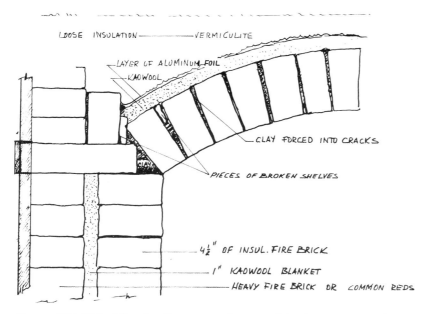

LOOSE INSULATION —— VERMICULITE

LAYER OF ALUMINUM FOIL
KAOWOOL

CLAY FORCED INTO CRACKS

PIECES OF BROKEN SHELVES

$4\frac{1}{2}$" OF INSUL. FIRE BRICK

1" KAOWOOL BLANKET

HEAVY FIRE BRICK OR COMMON REDS

Figure 108. This kiln detail exposes the use of body-stoneware clay as "wedge" material between standard bricks when used for arches. Also the use of bits of broken shelves to fill larger spaces. The wall detail shows again an effective use of the superb, but lightweight insulation Kaowool, which can be used within the walls and also on top of arches and kiln roofs.

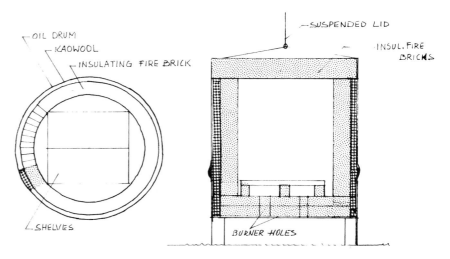

OIL DRUM
KAOWOOL
INSULATING FIRE BRICK
SHELVES

SUSPENDED LID
INSUL. FIRE BRICKS
BURNER HOLES

Figure 109. A small but effective kiln can be readily built into an *oil drum*. When the kiln is furnished with a suspended, counterweight lid, it can serve as an effective raku kiln. Using hard fire brick inside instead of insulators and doubling the Kaowool insulation the kiln can be used successfully for salt glazing. It is easily heated to even high temperature by a set of two or four medium size bunsen-burners.

Figure 110. A catenary arch kiln has the advantage of structural strength, if of modest size, it does not require heavy steel framing.

Figure 111. Wall detail using a relatively new material Kaowool. The product is a high-temperature ceramic fiber that can be used up to 2,300°F., with very little physical change, and at even higher temperatures in certain applications. It should be enthusiastically accepted by studio-type kiln builders as it saves weight and cost. The price per square foot is under $1.50 which is far less than insulating fire bricks, but the material furnishes an even better insulation in equal thicknesses. For kiln tops, this writer feels, *Kaowool* will become the standard material to insulate and cover arches with. The product is manufactured and marketed by the Babcock & Wilcox Refractories Division which has offices throughout the country.

Kaowool is available in the following basic products: Basic fiber bulk, blanket form, blocks, castables, ramming and tamping mixes, spray mixes, strip rope, and surface coating. The importance of this product for the small independent potter and his kilns is evident, and has therefore been presented here.

Figure 112. The layout of a kiln pattern on a concrete slab; the stacking space being determined by the size of kiln shelves.

Figure 113. Building the floor of the kiln. The space immediately under the floor will be filled with Kaowool scraps for insulation. The finished kiln floor will consist of *two* layers of heavy firebrick.

Figure 114. David Elliott, the builder, is ready to close the kiln for its first firing.

Figure 115. Dr. Foster Marlow, craftsman and art department chairman, views a similar kiln in the author's studio.

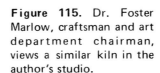

Figure 116. Stoneware bottle with flange neck, 12 inches, cotton ash glaze, by the author.

Chapter IV

The Nature of Creative Expression in Clay

CLAY AND FIRE

Someone once said that clay and fire wedded in a perfect marriage will create the sound of a bell. How true he was. It is indeed agreeable to discover that three of life's most vital elements are intimately involved in the making of pottery—earth, water, and fire. Each of these elements decidedly affects the outcome and provides the character of the finished product.

Earth-matter in the form of clay is at the heart of the self-expressive medium of ceramics. Given form, earth-matter becomes an object. Form emerges from clay as a tree emerges from a seed. A lump of clay contains the potentiality of a myriad of forms, but when one applies pressure to the plastic, pliable clay it responds to one's thoughts and ideas, and form emerges. That form eternalizes one's ideals of what pottery represents. In working with earth-matter, the artist-potter often experiences a fusion of the spiritual and the aesthetic. The author would like to maintain that few media of expression have the directness of clay when found, prospected, and prepared by oneself. As the author has aged in his craft, his ideals have radically changed. Novelties and gimmicks have little meaning. What matters is the integrity of the material, the *feel* for the clay—not in a puritanical sense but in that of artistic potential.

Clay is made plastic and responsive to the touch by the addition of water. Water provides the means by which clay becomes the pliable, responsive mud. More water will provide the potter with a softer body, and this body will bear the characteristics of softness when formed. Less water will make clay dry and harder to form and will also influence the final appearance of the piece. Water is used to *tame* clay, to make it obey one's aesthetic whims and wishes. In the final analysis, water is essential in making clay useful to the artist-potter.

Once a piece has been formed from clay, it must be dried and fired to achieve utility and permanence. As noted earlier, clay is basically decomposed rock, which when mixed with water and exposed to extreme heat returns to its rocklike state. A process which has taken nature millions of years to accomplish is reversed by the potter within a few hours by the use of fire. *Keramos*, burned earth, represents the essence of a medium stated in its name.

MOTIVATION IN CLAY

Craftsmen are a unique mixture of artists and technicians. This statement may offend the few who would like to retain the antiquated division between the crafts, and the so-called fine arts. The conflict is not one of utility versus pleasure, and certainly not one of the practical versus the aesthetic. Rather, the separation is essentially one concerning the materials used in one's art. All great craftsmen of the past and present have been and still are highly creative with their materials. Many of them surpass in creativity and expression a whole array of so-called "fine" artists. The problem has always been that a measure of artistry is prerequisite to any worthwhile success in a craft. "Pure" expression, as interpreted by a majority of critics and pseudo-experts, does not require a comparable knowledge and experience with an artistic medium of expression. In ceramics, no matter how often a pot is slapped with a piece of wood, cut, carved, stamped, or stepped

upon, it still has to be dried, fired, and finished. This includes many tasks of a technical character which self-selected "expressive" artists in many media consciously escape. And this is not meant to detract from the respect and admiration which should be accorded truly dedicated painters and sculptors.

Figure 118. Mrs. Vanderbilt Webb, president of the American Crafts Council discussing pottery with Mr. Charles Suckel, chairman of the art department at Southwest Texas State University, and a student.

Figure 117. Dark red stoneware bowl by Janet Leach, England. 8 inch diameter, black slip and white glaze decoration, reduction firing.

Here the attempt is to present in a condensed way the *innate* difference between the crafts and any other forms of creative activity. Possibly contrary to a common belief, this difference lies not in a degree of more or less creativity but in the requirements of the material. It is up to the artist to determine whether he is to become a craftsman or not. The crafts, including all media dealing with fiber, metal, clay, or whatever, have *constants* which are permanent. When these are applied to pottery, an understanding of the task occurs; a pot should be well *crafted*, it should appeal to the *touch*, it should be designed with *volume* in mind, and it should *function* well. When these constants are avoided or not observed, then the whole idea of a potter's craft is lost and becomes meaningless experimentation for the sake of novelty, gimmicks, and sensationalism.

In short, a craft can never be truly *all-expressive*. Some examples may go very far in personal expression, but there always remain the requirements of the material. These involve a number of deliberate *step-at-a-time* processes which are craftsmanship. The potter, to a far greater degree than he thinks, is a chemist-artist-technician, and when he becomes aware of all three levels of his activity, his products will gradually assume the essence of master work. Young ceramics students should be encouraged to carry their efforts always beyond the immediate, and never to be satisfied with early good results. They should go on with each project, step after step, venturing further than they had originally planned. This is the only way to achieve perfection in working with clay.

Sometimes new inspiration can be found in the old works of master craftsmen. KERAMOS is an attempt to shed new light upon age-old concepts and to translate these into twentieth century habits of systematic thinking. Much of the best pottery forms came from ancient Oriental potteries. Early Chinese potters endeavored in all their works to encompass the concept of "tao," which concerned the *life-spirit* inherent in all things. The achievement of "tao" in their art was the supreme challenge and the ultimate reward for the artist: its presence separated the master from the learner. In pottery, the pieces of the Tan'g and Sun'g dynasties have reflected this quality—especially when viewed in the original. Their aesthetic excellence as true expressions in the

77

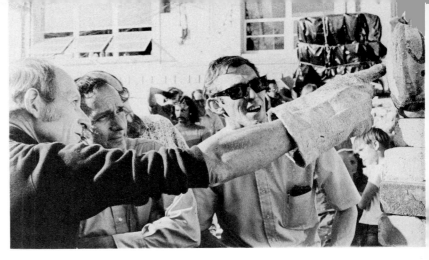

Figure 119. Potters Soldner, Ishmael Soto, and Kirby Benson discussing effects during one of Mr. Soldners many demonstrations.

Figure 120. Internationally acclaimed master potter Wilhelm Kage from Sweden. Mr. Kage spent nine years in mainland China studying Tan'g and Sun'g glazes, and is one of the very few pioneers of modern stoneware in Europe.

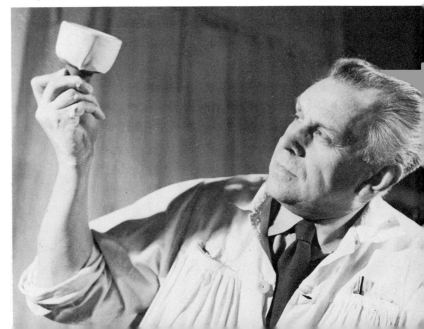

particular medium of clay offer superb examples. Many Western potters have visited the Orient, and some have come back Orientalized. To find inspiration in these vessels is useful, but to imitate them becomes a thankless task because their quality and excellence largely depended upon particular clays, degrees of heat, and other factors which can hardly be achieved in our modern times.

It is realistic to accept the fact that the creation of pottery is not all romance. The search for wonder in any craft is often *hard work*. There is magic in working with clay, but dedication, self-honesty, and persistence are necessary in doing so. Common sense and new concepts will go far to provide motivation, and new opportunities for achievement will arise from new approaches. The true craftsman is always giving: in fact, one might say that he is a *go-giver* rather than a *go-getter*. His personal drive to pursue his goals is the *go*; and, guided by his philosophy of self-realization, he *gives* of his talent to those who appreciate his work. When craftsmen call themselves rejected and misunderstood, they as often as

Figure 121. A craft can never be truly *all-expressive*. Some examples may go very far in personal expression, but there always remain the requirements of the material.

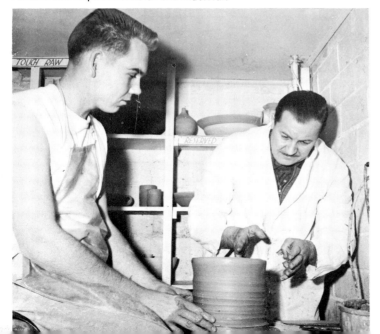

not are married to their own narrow conceptions of art and are divorced from the real world of life. Most master-craftsmen have not been "understood" during their developmental stages, but have nevertheless persisted and kept on *giving*. They found their dreams, desires, and goals sufficient to sustain their energies in an ever-continuous search for true expression. Often a master-craftsman is accused of commercialism when he attempts to reach the public with his products. How else can most craftsmen cope with their daily expenses? As in any other profession, a craftsman is also entitled to his full measure of economic reward. If the buyer is aesthetically pleased and as a result of the transaction has grown in appreciation of art, then he has received something the artist has *given*. A ball of clay does not necessarily become a better pot because it is more expensive than another ball of clay. The craftsman must create from the material and whatever its cost, the appreciator will still be the getter—the artist the giver. Last but not least, any sale of one's work represents a considerable recognition of the artist in terms of the buyer who also happens to be the appreciator.

Finally, the artist-craftsman, whether beginner or advanced, has to believe in himself and his material. He has to embrace pottery as the particular form of his contribution to his environment. This has nothing to do with the often misguided missionary spirit of beatniks and pseudo-artists. It has everything to do with the choice and establishment of an individual's personal goals of excellence in a craft. Without personal *specific goals* modern psychology tells us, there can be no *personal achievement*. Ninety-eight percent of all people have no consciously set goals and live their lives in a mold of day-to-day opportunism. Their lives are dominated by the social patterns of race, state, and immediate environment. These are the *doing-as-the-Joneses-do* all over the world. Many who finally establish some goals change them so often that they turn into vague daydreams. Artists have always claimed to be different from ordinary citizens: at their best, they should be different members of society because they should be citizens *with a goal*. W.I. Thomas, one of the deans of American sociologists, presented one of the theories basic in social science: "If men define situations as real, they become real in their consequences."

For a long time this writer has shared the belief that a self-confident student will perform better than one who is not. The Thomas theory might be interpreted to say: set your goals, believe in them and your own ability to achieve them, and you *will* achieve them. A person so motivated in any field will succeed. Once an individual has allocated a meaning to a situation (or goal), his consequent behavior (search) and the consequences of that behavior are determined by that ascribed meaning.

From the foregoing paragraphs, one can assume that to a certain degree motivation in the crafts and motivation in general possess a pattern which can be followed. Philosophers of art generally agree that all normal individuals are born with a certain amount of aesthetic sensitivity, and that whether one becomes an artist or not depends upon how far one develops this innate aesthetic potential. The history of art is filled with examples of late starters in artistic development. It is never too late to straighten out one's thoughts and guide them into new and fruitful patterns. In psychology it is more and more recognized that we use only a fraction of our immense mind-potential. In consideration of these factors it becomes possible to ask: does such a thing as a success formula for craftsmen exist? Yes, I believe that it does, but the formula is not simple or easy to follow, but it works 100 percent of the time. It is a highly personal *individualized idealization* meaning *self-discipline*—a most difficult thing to achieve. To use the formula is the prerogative of the artist-craftsman who believes in emotional involvement with his work (though it will also work in any profession and is found throughout the country in many self-improvement courses). For the artist with his search for true expression, innovation, and adventure, however, it is tailor-made. The artist is a natural dreamer who imagines and visualizes things but who seldom organizes any effort for his own benefit. The formula could be called, if any name is necessary, *organized effort*. It involves the following: (1) a *goal* (or a sincere desire for success in pottery) *plus* (2) *contact* (or knowing more about pottery than most others) *plus* (3) *self* (or self-criticism and self-evaluation) *plus* (4) *persistence* (or constant practice, both technical and aesthetic)—all combined equal *success*.

Figure 122. Potter Clyde E. Burt from Ohio holds one of his specialties, a wax-resist decorated, large stoneware urn.

Figure 123. Victor Spinski, head of the ceramics department at the University of Delaware standing beside one of his clay structures. Mr. Spinski is well known for his advanced techniques in construction and silkscreen decor on ceramic surfaces.

Figure 124. "Suminagashi" (floating black stain) plate. Yutaka Kondo, City College of Fine Arts, Kyoto, Japan. The effect was accidentally discovered by professor Kondo when working with different methods of black and white slip decoration. Accidently he happened to drip black slip onto the white surface in an unwanted place; in disgust he blew at it and noticed the interesting pattern.

1. *Goal*: Each potter should sincerely analyze his potential and set his goals. He should know in detail what it is that he wants to achieve. These details should be written down and used from time to time to check progress. In his imagination he should view himself as having already achieved his goals. This is best accomplished by setting aside a specific time each day. Ten or twenty minutes are sufficient. If he has no time, he should make the time, for this is the most significant step he can take in his career. He should withdraw into a quiet room and relax—even to the point of slipping into a drowsy state while meditating upon what successes he has had. Nothing succeeds more than success itself and it is good to remind oneself occasionally of successes already achieved. One's

mind may attempt to wander off, but it should be brought back, kept on course, should concentrate on final goals, the desired criteria to be achieved, and should then consider problems from every possible standpoint. Above all, the potter in his imagination needs to see the job as *already successfully accomplished*. In such meditation the artist is using the powers of *concentration, idealization,* and *visualization*. One should use them every day at the same time, if possible, until one has achieved major goals. The results of such controlled, concentrated imagination will be a deep desire followed by dynamic action. First, one may become convinced by repeated self-suggestion that one can succeed and then develop a strong self-confidence: and as the self-confidence grows it will reflect itself in such a way as to constantly attract success. (There are no limits to one's imagination, it is just as easy to imagine oneself to be the Number One potter of the country as it is to imagine oneself to be the Number One potter of the town.)

2. *Contact*: No one has ever succeeded by bluffing himself into a position or job because to succeed generally involves a lot of *hard work*. For the craftsman-potter it means that he must know more about his specific field in pottery than anyone else. He may be an expert on raku, as is Paul Soldner, or on any other form or combination of forms of pottery. The Wildenheins are known for their stonewares, the Natzlers for their fine glazes, and Henry Varnum Poor for his low-fire earthenwares. Now is the time of specialization and this is a fact the young potter who wishes to succeed must understand. He must acquire all the knowledge possible from wherever he can get it. This does not necessarily mean a college degree. In fact, some of the poorest potters have the highest degrees, and some of the best—such as Voulkos and Soldner—came from other fields. Contact simply means the acquisition of all knowledge, theoretical or practical, that will enable one to produce the best in his craft. One can acquire this knowledge from books, libraries, courses in schools and colleges, and from acquaintances with the same interests. The skills must be practiced. It is a fact in modern psychology that the nervous system does not know the difference between vividly imagined experience and "real" experience. Therefore, it is possible to practice mentally

through creative imagination. When relaxing in your chair, close your eyes, see yourself throwing the clay on the potter's wheel, throw tall cylinders, stop in your imagination and cut the cylinders in half. Note where the heavy wall spots are. Throw again, and correct the heavy spots in the cylinder walls. Cut them apart again. Do this for ten minutes for a period of several weeks. Your real throwing will improve immensely. Musicians have used mental practice consciously or unconsciously for ages. It would be impossible to memorize each finger movement of a piano score: the player must rely upon his subconscious power to execute the score. He must *think* the score through before he even starts to practice on the instrument. Potters young and old can do the same. Use mental practice.

3. *Self*: The artist must know more about himself than the ordinary citizen if he is to claim "self-expression." *Know thyself* for the craftsman means that he must be his first and foremost critic. Such self-evaluation will enable him to recognize his shortcomings as a craftsman and artist and turn them into valuable assets. Picasso during his life has never ceased to develop new styles, and as an innovator never stooped to gimmickry and novelty for novelty's sake. A potter must love his craft without unduly falling in love with his objects. This would blind the critic within. A craftsman who makes such "beautiful" pots that he can't stand to sell them usually is too blind to see his own inconsistencies. Self-evaluation is self-awareness.

4. *Persistence*: One must grow and persist in the craft if one is to increase in experience. Constant practice and a search for new forms of expression within the limits of the material are almost sure to bring success. If a craftsman persistently enters his work in exhibitions, he should do so on an impersonal basis and not become disappointed at rejections. Exhibits are selected by human beings, all humans make mistakes, and few of them are really qualified to "judge" in the strictest sense of the word. Their selections are based upon *their level of understanding*. More often than not pots rejected in one show have been accepted in another show by another judge. One should keep track of how many shows one has entered, of how many accepted one's entry, and of how much noticeable improvement one is making from year to year. Business

Figure 125. *The General,* stoneware sculpture by Stig Lindberg, Gustafsberg, Sweden, coll. of Swedish National Museum, Stockholm.

Figure 126. Potters must wear many hats. They must be technicians, chemists, engineers, businessmen, and above all, humans and artists. Potter Steve Zavorski, Jr., from St. Louis, Mo. is trying on one of his own pots.

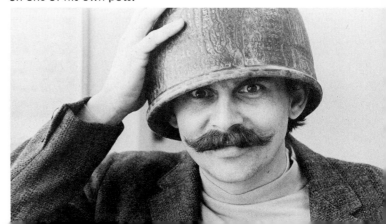

in America uses the law of averages. If the potter-artist persists in learning, practicing, and producing, the law of averages should work to make success inevitable. In summary:

1. You must know where you are in order to know where you want to go next.

2. Believe that you have something to say in clay, and in time you will say it.

3. Belief is faith, and faith consists of the thoughts in your mind.

4. The thoughts and ideas in your mind can be influenced by suggestion.

5. Meditation and imagination are strong vehicles of self-suggestion.

6. Don't change course all the time, persist in what you are doing long enough for results to appear.

7. Mental practice strengthens your power of imagination and is a potent form of self-suggestion.

Figure 128. Large, thrown branch bottle, 28 inches tall, by James McKinnell. Matte copper glaze with wax resist and iron brush decoration.

Figure 127. Have gourds, seedpods, and other natural forms, been created by potters? Many suggest ceramic forms growing out of the organic character of all things in nature living or dead.

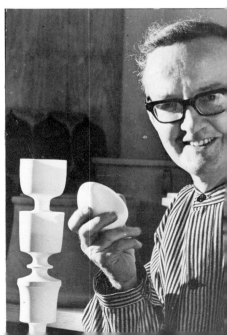

Figure 129. Which came first, the egg or the stand? Sweden's Stig Lindberg seems to be asking the question. Mr. Lindberg is internationally known for his grotesque, humorous philosophy expressed in most of his ceramic objects.

THE PAST

In the past clay has served man from the cradle to the grave. There is no doubt that the making of clay objects began as soon as man settled down to an agrarian existence. Although no one is sure exactly when this happened, some crude earthenware objects have been found that are believed to be 9,000 years old. Through these crude bowls man imparted to later generations the spirit of his time. Clay was pliable when wet, conforming to the pressure of his hands. He found clay sympathetic to his needs to symbolize reality. Early societies worshipped death, and thus tombs and burial places which have been unearthed have yielded enormous numbers of artifacts which are mostly made of clay. Fetiches and symbols were necessary items which aided one in the achievement of emotional stability. These items, being considered sacred, always represented the best in expression and craftsmanship of the society. In such objects the character of a culture has been skillfully imprinted in the medium of clay. Never would early man just do "something" with his clay, the material was reverent, the meaning of the object produced was deep. One should hope that our experience in clay may breathe the same intent. Perhaps not as accomplished in one's skill as one would like to be, one still attempts to advance further beyond the "something" into a purposeful experimentation with form and material.

Oriental potters expressed the quality of clay superbly. Chinese ceramics of the Tan'g and Sun'g dynasties have the aesthetic appeal of works of art. The forming, glazing, and firing proclaim a magnificent skill and unprecedented beauty along with their native Oriental character. Although, according to Oriental philosophy, imitation was a way of learning, the stoneware pieces of the Sun'g period display an inexplicable individuality which is anchored in a thorough understanding of the craft and its aesthetic criteria. From the third century A.D. the Chinese knew the secrets of porcelain manufacture and reduction-firing. Their thirst for a natural approach to ceramics resulted in the treasured celadon glazes and their beautiful copper reds. In their works there can be sensed the source of clay, or the *mother rock.*

In our own Mediterranean culture the heritage of pottery is rich and manifold. Egyptians knew the methods of glazing even before

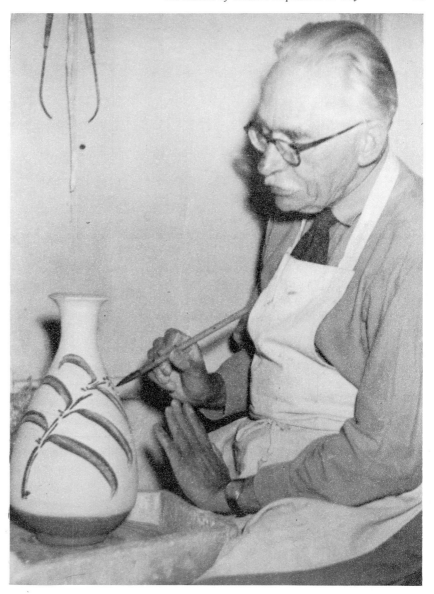

Figure 130. Bernard Leach, England, at his St. Ives Pottery demonstrating brush-work on one of his porcelain bottles. Mr. Leach is internationally recognized as the dean of modern potters.

Figure 131. Frans Wildenhain the noted potter from the Rochester Institute of Design and the author walking down a quiet, wooded alley on the campus of the State University of Pennsylvania.

Figure 132. There are moments of reflection in a potter's life. Inspiration comes easier when sitting on a "potted" stool, at a "potted" table sipping wine from a "potted" chalice as potter Raymond Grimm demonstrates in his backyard in Portland, Oregon. All pieces are stoneware fired to cone 9.

history was recorded. The Egyptian potters desired to create a contrast to the burning colors of the sun and sandy desert, and to pour a bit of the blue color of the Nile into the huts and houses of the nobles and nomads. This desire resulted in the brilliant copper blues and greens one now admires. But the potters of Egypt also found inspiration in their own backyards. Much of their forms reflect plants which could be found along the banks of the Nile: predominantly papyrus, acanthus, palm, and almond forms.

In Babylon, along the Tigris and Euphrates rivers, clay began to serve in a new way. The writing in soft clay tablets which could be stored indicated a new era of man. On the island of Crete the potter was a craftsman of consequence. The potteries of *Kamares*, dating back some 2,000 years before Christ, express superb craftsmanship and the fresh care-free spirit of a happy people. A society which felt no need for fortifications and which was drenched with a mythology concerning the secrets of life could therefore build palaces. It was only natural that the patterns of their environment would dominate their products. From the ripe pregnant perimeter of storage vessels to the slender beauty of perfume jars the potters wedded form and function into one.

The pottery of the American Indians evokes a feeling for strange fables and tales. Many pieces are like the sounds of unknown instruments, sounds caused by the winds blowing through the deep gorges of the Rockies and the Andes. Their forms are bold and full of vigor. Many motifs were inspired by their religious legends, are abstractions of natural phenomena, and have deep connections with their religious rituals.

As the concept of the fine arts developed on the European continent, the making of pottery became more and more associated with the production of useful items. Commercial factors were found to affect the potter who then began, as a producing craftsman, to depend upon his production for a livelihood. The frilly beauty of the Italian majolicas, the French painted porcelains, and the simplicity of English pottery are all products of the practical age. Once in a while, provided the proper background was present, a Lucca della Robia would come along and elevate clay to a lofty position.

More recently, late in the nineteenth century as a vague opposi-

84

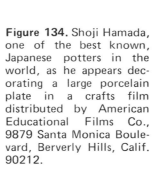

Figure 133. Ceramics designer Tyra Lundgren, Sweden. Miss Lundgren has been for many years a co-worker of Wilhelm Kage at Gustafsberg in Sweden and is especially famous for her interpretation of bird life in heavily grogged stoneware clays.

THE PRESENT

The importance of any craftsman in a given society depends largely upon the opinions which that society formed toward craftsmen as a group. In the United States, caused by an extended period of prosperity, the hand-crafted object has been illuminated and presently appears in a new light of acceptance. The crafts along with other art forms, have become academically acceptable and in some cases are warmly embraced in specialized and humanistic programs. Certainly, this recognition of aesthetic values, as

tion to the approaching machine age, the concept of the artist-craftsman was born. In Europe, and especially in England, this movement became important: the hand-made object versus the machine-made object. The attempt to slow down machine production failed. The objectives of the Morrison movement were erroneous, and the potter remained a curiosity among his fellow men. It was not until many accepted the concept of the craftsman-designer that he was chosen to play a different role in the twentieth century. In our time the craftsman should not compete, he should explore, he should pioneer form, he should be the developer of taste, he should be an experimenter. In this way he should supplement rather than oppose industry. In this direction the new craftsman-designer is gaining a measure of significance. Today the industry produces for the masses, but its forms are more often than not inspired by the craftsman-designer. Often industry is seeking this inspiration. In his work shop the artist-potter continues to search, dream, resolve, wish, and explore the wonder that is clay.

Figure 134. Shoji Hamada, one of the best known, Japanese potters in the world, as he appears decorating a large porcelain plate in a crafts film distributed by American Educational Films Co., 9879 Santa Monica Boulevard, Berverly Hills, Calif. 90212.

Figure 135. Cherry-blossom wine case, old type of "Kiyomizu" ware from the middle of the Edo period. Red clay body with transparent glaze and white slip trailing. Eight inches high.

represented by the hand-made object, have not happened over night, but have become apparent through an ever increasing exposure of the public to the potters art during the educational process. It is a fact that the number of ceramics courses offered for academic credits have tripled in the past five years in the nation's colleges. Ceramic arts conferences, annual, or one-shot affairs, are multiplying like coat hangers in a forgotten closet. This wave of renewed interest has opened the doors of acclaimed galleries to the potter. In the past such galleries considered pottery a *minor art* hardly to be accepted in their hallowed halls. In Asia, old master potters such as Shoji Hamada have been declared living, national monuments of the state.

Not all of these new developments are entirely beneficial to the craft. The sudden shift from apprenticeship training in private art schools and academies to classroom instruction in *pot-making* are the cause of numerous handicaps which are often rationalized to be of benefit to self-expression and artistic freedom. The attitudes expressed by many potters in regard to technique, function and aesthetic expression cover every imaginable clay form and are poles apart. Almost all potters have in the past concerned themselves primarily with wheel-thrown shapes, great numbers are now turning more and more to slab construction which allows more form freedom for the individual. At the other hand, there still exists a sizable number of individual craftsmen who believe in a certain amount of utility and insist that only the usable pot which is also handsome can take on that special dimension which is considered art. The Bauhaus at Weimer and later at Dessau in Germany, trained its students according to European traditions in the technique of the craft, but also *added* a highly creative environment which encouraged, and enhanced self-expression. The realization of its leaders that skill definitely had its place in the framework of artistic training brought about a wedding of *know-how* and *aesthetic sensitivity* toward the material. Today in numerous classrooms which expound the history of art the ideals of the Bauhaus are discussed and discussed, but in practice, the student returns to his so-called *studio-class* only to be subjected to the same old search for tricks and gimmicks. On the surface we are at the present experiencing an era of a *cult of ugliness.* Any organized society always chooses its own heroes, it produces in all fields an elite of stars. In the area of the crafts, the number of those who are attempting in any way to achieve instant fame and who are no more than glorified experimenters seem to be dwindling. Nevertheless, there still are some whose successes flare up like the glow of a flaming star, heralded as innovators by quasi-sophisticated writers in the professional press, only to be forgotten after the next two issues.

What really has been lost in such hurried-up preparation is the essential *know-how, know-why,* and *know-what,* all three criteria being pertinent to true self-expression. Furthermore, an intense, accumulated knowledge of the craft has been lost, a knowledge which included form and material, both of which are absolutely necessary for a truly artistic production. Pottery is a process in sequence of developing a natural material, it requires a long time and involves the making of thousands of pots to really understand and to perceive. Such can hardly be achieved in the short time one semester offers, but when undertaken consciously, gradually an appreciation develops for the material, *for its potentials and its limitations.* It is the limitations as much as the potentials which in final analysis influence the creative process. It is the physicality of the craft that is so pleasing, from which the student can learn through his hands, his eyes, and his skin those subtle things about pottery that are hard to learn through his brain. It is possible in this way to develop a sense of life, of the world, of the elements earth, water and fire, along with a beneficial reverence for clay. Problems always arise when the desire to express ideas as visualized by the mind are accompanied by a lack of know-how and an *every-thing-goes* attitude is accepted in the name of creativity as a way out. It should be clear to the student from the previous statement that he first strive for a completeness in the craft. Once the craft is thoroughly understood, provided that the student has something to express, he will have the means at his hand to express it.

To avoid any misunderstanding by the reader, the above paragraph was not intended to negate the importance of originality and original contributions to the craft. But, it is important in this framework, as in life, that a person stands on his own two feet and not live parasitically copying the latest fad around him. The question that is being posed, is that, whether consciously or not, many students are copying each other rather than objectifying their own internalized concepts.

THE PRODUCING POTTER

On the continents of Europe and Asia potters are well aware of the selling aspects of handmade objects. Without sacrificing their

Figure 136. A "Teaburi," old type handwarmer of Kiyomizu ware, middle of the Edo period in Japan. Made from a white clay body which is skillfully cut out to expose the burning charcoal. Crackle glaze with red, silver, gold and green overglaze decoration. 12 inches long.

Figure 137. Don Schaumburg, Arizona State University, with a number of his pots. Photo by Jan Young.

Figure 138. Pre-Columbian clay figure originally used in religious ceremonies. From the coll. of Mr. & Mrs. Charles Suckle, San Marcos, Texas.

Figure 139. Vessel, handformed. American Indians attached significance to all details of the design.

aesthetic standards their common goal can be seen in satisfying prospective customers. These significant artist-craftsmen are not embarrassed nor repulsed by innuendos of commercialism. Most of them feel needed, fulfilling the needs of society as makers of beautiful objects and as artists. They are convinced that whatever rewards are bestowed upon them through their sales are deserved and represent the proper recognition the society owes them. An increasing number serves industry in the capacity of designers and artistic advisors. Bernard Leach's pottery shop in St. Ives, England, is perhaps the best example of a small, producing pottery shop where highest standards of design prevailed. After an extended stay in Japan, which finally led to a warm friendship of Mr. Leach with some of Japan's leading potters including Shoji Hamada, Leach felt the need to implement his desires for high standards of "handcraftmanship" and design of usable items in England. By establishing the St. Ives shop he successfully accomplished the ideal of most studio-potters, to operate their own pot-shop. It enabled him to offer his refined products to a much wider circle of public, while on a limited basis, he was able to train a number of young craftsmen in an awareness of high standards in functional pottery. The great number of pieces coming annually from the Leach pottery are ample proof of his professed convictions that functional items can be handsome and that there is no need to sacrifice one's aesthetic integrity in order to produce salable pots.

In almost every country, on all continents, people are earning their livelihood by hand-making of ceramic wares. Many of these individuals are folk-artists, but few if any, are aware of such high-strung classifications. The great majority continue within traditional lines in skill and design and consider themselves, in a rather classical sense specialized, manual workers. Once in a while someone breaks through the surface and acquires acclaim as an artist in his field. It is only recently that the charm and fascination with primitive working methods brought many to the attention of the West. Their honesty and humility toward the craft, and their natural sensitivity for clay are beyond reproach and are reflected in many of their products.

THE SILVERTON IDEA

In the United States, as in other parts of the world, a limited number of small pottery shops are presently operated with varying success. Nevertheless, any significant reports and meaningful advice concerning the establisment of such one-man potteries are lacking. A young potter interested in the establishment of his own shop is usually on his own and those who do succeed do so in spite of the many surprise problems that are connected with the task. It is obvious from what has been said in this book, that such shops are needed and can be very successful. No large investments of monies are involved. Actually, this is one of the great advantages the craftsman has over most other persons planning a business venture, he can start alone without employees, he himself masters the whole process, and his total investment in terms of tools and materials is usually small enough that it can be afforded by anyone. One of the ideas which finally led to this book was to actually establish such a one-man shop, study the problems which arise carefully, and pass any useful knowledge on to the interested reader. It is an attempt to correct a neglected area in the education of our craftsmen. For me, the idea eventually materialized in Silverton.

The objectives were clear, first to find a place which appeared promising for such a venture, secondly, establish the pot-shop and carefully tabulate all financial, organizational, and aesthetic factors, thirdly operate the pottery long enough to establish credibility for the resulting data, and fourth, make an attempt to present the results in readable form. Once the objectives were clarified and accepted an arbitrary checklist of items was devised to serve as a sort of guide for the selection of an area and a community which would give some indication of a possibility for success.

1. Area and community?

2. Location within the community?

3. Acceptance by the community?

4. Technical factors; materials and transportation?

Figure 140. Traditional shapes are still produced at the Jamestown, Virginia pottery. Pottery and glass represented some of the earliest products manufactured by the settlers of the New World.

Figure 141. Early American jug. Stoneware with natural slip glaze.

5. Sales potential?

6. Potential for expansion?

7. Investment needed for start?

It became imperative to answer all questions with candid honesty and to do this, because of the approximity the search for the right place was concentrated upon the mountain states of the central Rockies. After several trips to Colorado the signals that promised possible success were located in Silverton, a mining community on the western slope. A special, week long trip was arranged to Silverton during the summer of 1966, to study the community and all possibilities regarding a future pottery there closely. Contacts were made with significant people in the community, available facilities were surveyed, movement patterns of visitors who would turn into customers were recorded.

1. Silverton is a community rich in history and scenic beauty nestled at the center of the rugged San Juan Mountains in Southwestern Colorado. An estimated 850 people live at Silverton's 9,302 feet elevation the year around, which is still the site of several working mines. It is also the Northern

Figure 142. Tea set with cookie jar, stoneware, ash glaze and dark, olive celadon glaze, by the author.

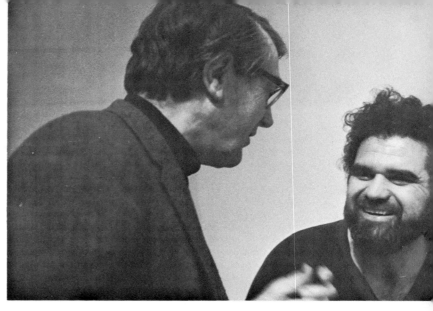

Figure 143. Frans Wildenhein noted potter from the Rochester Institute of Art and Jerry Rothman, State University of Iowa exchange ideas regarding pottery.

terminus of the last regularly scheduled narrow gauge passenger train in the land, and each summer it is visited and entertains thousands of vacationing visitors.

2. An old house brought to Silverton from the nearby ghost town Eureka was located for sale only 80 yards from the trainstop on Blairstreet. The house was purchased with ample space around it to assure room for later expansion. In the meantime the front room of the house would serve as the store while the back was used for working space.

3. By contacting the editor of the local paper and a number of businessmen, the author was assured of genuine acceptance and encouragement by the townspeople. It should be obvious to any craftsman that the contact with local individuals should be made at an earliest stage and may turn out to be the most important factor for long term success. Their direct help in locating properties and advice concerning the community are invaluable. A good point for the craftsman to start off a meaningful conversation is simply to assure these people of one's complete cooperation with the community. Good public relations are important for any one starting a

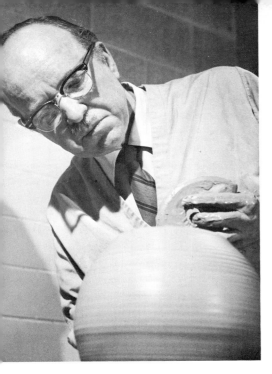

Figure 144. Karl Martz, noted for his many contributions to pottery in the field of glazes. He is a constant contributor through *Ceramics Monthly Magazine* and is professor of ceramics at Indiana University.

new venture, whether it be a single craftsman or a giant, national corporation.

4. Some materials useful in the making of pottery were found in local mines and lumber mills. Local ores and ashes from the lumber mills are used extensively in the potteries' glazes. This availability of ores and ashes lead to the decision to specialize in ore and ash glazes, which proved later to be an effective, additional selling point especially for collectors of glazed pottery. Transportation was assured by daily trucks operated by the Rio Grande Transport Co.

5. Each summer more than 100,000 persons visit Silverton by train or by car, according to U.S. statistics if only 1% of the visitors would prove to be potential buyers, a one-man pottery could scarecely supply the demand. One of the hopes of the author for Silverton is that eventually, the pottery will serve, as the Leach pottery in England, in the training of promising young potters in this country. When this phase arrives then the store can become an effective outlet for all students in participation.

6. Expansion of the pottery is possible in several directions, in its physical size there is enough room to satisfy future needs, but perhaps even more significant with the aid of the community the pottery may someday be established as a study center.

7. Every serious student of the craft eventually accumulates enough tools and equipment to furnish a one-man shop. The question of investments relates more in regard to buildings, facilities and the kiln. In the case of Silverton, savings and a small personal loan were sufficient. Shelves, store counters, lighting and storage space were built by the author with the help of his family and friends. In fact, the project became family orientated as every member of the family was caught in a spontaneous enthusiasm including that the shop meant a lengthy stay in the mountains for every one each summer.

The Silverton Mountain Pottery has now been in operation four full summers. It opens every June 1st, and closes on August 30th. It has proven very successful in every respect. Three special subject areas have been recognized and isolated in the endeavor and should be of great interest to every potential craftsman. As expected, these three factors are being neglected in the preparation of craftsmen in most of our colleges. The criteria which made Silverton successful are a reasonable, but firm *shop-rhythm*, a

Figure 145. Les Lawrence, a young potter at work, Arizona State University. Mr. Lawrence gained his early experience in pottery from the author. Photo by Jan Young.

basic awareness and knowledge of a *craftsman's-public-relations*, and *craftsmans-economics*. At a very early stage of the project it became apparent that what was needed most was some degree of knowledge regarding these criteria, and that these factors were vital to the final, economically sound set-up of a self-sustaining small pot-shop.

SHOP RHYTHM

It is important to establish at the outset a *natural succession* of tasks to be performed, a sort of *sequence of operations* that should be kept throughout the working day. The standardization of the work process will always benefit the shop, it represents an economization of the shop and will avoid waste of materials and time. A shop-rhythm can be arranged with time or individual operations in mind. Man has always been a creature of his habits, and a deliberate shop-rhythm represents no more than a predetermined effort to establish good studio habits. The Silverton Mountain Pottery functions well using a *time* based shop-rhythm.

Monday — throwing of flat shapes

Tuesday — throwing of high shapes

Wednesday — mixing and pugging of clay. Clean-up.

Thursday — glazing and preparation of glazes

Friday — creative day

Saturday — office work and shipping

This shop-rhythm is followed by a firing schedule which follows through regardless of shop activity. The kiln is tended to while work in the shop goes on. The kiln is fired three times per week with a 24 hour firing cycle. Another form of shop-rhythm, which the author observed in many European potteries, can be devised around the particular involved in the making of pottery.

Clay preparation and general shop clean-up.

Throwing and forming.

Figure 146. Tranquility surrounds the Silverton Mountain Pottery early in the morning. The structure was brought into Silverton by a Hollywood movie company from the nearby ghost town Eureka, the kiln shed is new and has been added by the author in 1967.

Figure 147. As the sun rises over Kendall Mountain, the notorious Blair Street becomes a crowded place. Tourists arriving by the Rio Grande, narrow gauge, railroad swarm through the town, the busy time for the pottery begins.

Figure 148. Everybody likes to watch a potter. The author throwing pots on a portable wheel on the porch demonstrating the technique to curious onlookers.

Figure 149. The main display area in the pottery shop. During the summer of 1974 more than 20 thousand persons visited the pottery.

First finishing—bisque firing.

Glazing, decorating—glaze firing.

Finishing and shipping.

Office and general work.

The studio-potter should limit his desire to make too many *one-of-a-kind* pieces, he is most successful when working in repetitive quantities. To illustrate this concept; a reasonable number of bowls have been thrown on the potters wheel at one time (perhaps a day's work), they are similar, they represent the style of the artist-potter, but they are not exactly alike. No machine-like efficiency is possible, nor is it desirable. As soon as they are dry, the bowls are cleaned with steel wool to remove the burr and bisque fired, glazed, decorated, glaze fired, checked for defects and delivered to the display area. When the original number of bowls is large enough, each task becomes a part of a rhythm excluding boredom because of the change of activity in each operation, and economizing time within each operation. The shelves of a one-man pot-shop are always filled with *series* of items either drying or waiting for the next step in the sequence. Of course, it should be clearly understood, that by neccesity shop-rhythms will vary with the individual pottery depending on many factors including size of the pottery, location, and personal preference. The Kato family of potters in the town Tajimi, Japan, produces approximately 20,000

Figure 150. Production pottery from the famous Leach shop in St. Ives, England.

Figure 151. Angelo Garcio, Kansas State University. A beautiful stoneware tea pot. Reduction fired to cone 8, rust red, matte glaze.

Figure 152. The author throwing a large vessel at his Silverton Mountain Pottery. The clay body is composed from 30% of local, coarse, low fire clay and 70% Colorado fire clay.

rice bowls every 45 days. A well thought out shop-rhythm is vital to such an operation. The pottery has been over one hundred years in the same family and is now operated by two brothers, their wives, and aging parents. Both brothers are also renowned artists in their craft. In final analysis, as mentioned before, the term shop-rhythm is just another name for *organized effort*.

A CRAFTSMAN'S PUBLIC RELATIONS

Once a shop is set-up and is expected to operate within sound profit margins, the craftsman must sell. Whatever his philosophy concerning his work and his product may be, he must now attempt to convey that philosophy to potential buyers effectively enough to entice or incite them to make the final purchase. Few if any, of the craftsmen who operate their own shops have succeeded by riding on the lofty horse of *self-explanatory-art*. The "I don't owe you an explanation" attitude simply is not applicable to a craftshop. Buyers of handcrafted items are also appreciators, they are interested and want to know everything connected with the crafted piece, its message, technique and material. *This in fact is the greatest advantage the studio-potter has over his competition.* He has made the item, he knows more about it than any other individual and he must be willing to pass this information on to the customer. The craftsman depends largely upon a prestige market, that is, the strongest incentive to buy a handcrafted item lies in the buyer's belief that the ownership of this item will culturally, or otherwise enhance the owner's standing. The craftsman must attempt to understand the flow of thought in the customer's mind. It is only a small jump of imagination from the phrase "I bought a handmade piece of pottery" to "and I met the man who made it." The above represent clearly the strongest selling tool for the artist potter, his personal involvement in the act of selling whenever possible. Perhaps, there are many ways this personal touch can be extended and brought across to potential buyers, two proven ways besides the actual presence of the artist are here presented:

1. *Personal identification* of the artist with the shop and every item in it. In Silverton two experiments were carried out under strict supervision, one involving the selling of pottery

made by a well-known artist who was not present in the shop, and another experiment involving the effects of the artist's signature on the buying public. In the first experiment excellent stoneware pieces were accepted on commision basis and displayed side by side with pottery made in Silverton. The result of which was that people would pick up the objects, often laudibly admire their form, but return them to the shelf as soon as they noticed that the signature was not that of the potter in residence. In the second experiment two hundred items of each were mingled on the shelves. The pieces were made by the same potter but half of them were signed by neatly stamping a K in a small circle, and half of them were simply signed with a 4 penny nail by three letters engraved into the moist clay. The result of this rather unscientific survey was astonishing. Pots who carried the signature made with nail outsold the stamped pots at the rate of seven to one. Somehow the customer connected the scribbled, personal marks with the personal integrity of the artist. Almost one hundred percent replied to the question of why they liked the signed pot better with answers tantamount with the personal honesty of the artist. Therefore, a shop should directly and indirectly attempt to carry the personal image of the artist and heavily reflect his philosophies. Much can be achieved by the way the pottery is displayed, lighting, and services offered.

2. Perhaps the second strongest sales stimulators are well organized studio-demonstrations and shop *tie-ins*. These can be arranged in many different ways, and always must be especially fitted to the situation at hand. In the Silverton Mountain Pottery a window is being kept open which allows an unobstructed view of the actual shop area. The arrangement has proven effective and practical as it does not interfere with the normal flow of work in the shop. Such living display windows actually provide one of the best ways of shop *tie-in* to a well planned store area providing exhibition space.

Where space is available, raku techniques suit themselves excellently for demonstrations and are good sales stimulators. Almost all people always enjoy watching a throwing potter

Figure 153. Alfred Saidl, Austria, stylized pitcher, earthenware, matte dark brown glaze.

Figure 154. Production ware designed by Stig Lindberg, Sweden, produced by A.B. Gustafsberg Fabriker, of which Mr. Lindberg is art director and artistic adviser.

Figure 155. White stoneware sculpture "From the Swanelake," by Britt Ingrid Person, Sweden.

Figure 156. Candleholders, stoneware, white brown and gold, by Lisa Larson, Gustafsberg Studio, Sweden.

on his wheel, at the Silverton Mountain Pottery the author always keeps plenty of clay at hand always ready to demonstrate. European and Asian potters are also master salesmen and utilize freely the magic that surrounds the potter's wheel. Many offer studio tours as shop tie-ins. These masters of the craft also realize, nevertheless, that their strongest sales stimulator is simply their presence. They do involve themselves directly in the business of selling. Their opinions regarding the product are taken at face value as that of an expert, after all they have made the object.

3. Large corporations have often elaborated on very specific policies concerning advertising. Astronomical sums of money go to Madison Avenue advertising tycoons to be employed in advertising and sales campaigns. The story that a good salesman can sell a refrigerator to an eskimo for his igloo is not as farfetched as some would think. On a much smaller scale, the artist craftsman in his shop shares many of the same problems. In Silverton, it was observed very early that most buyers appreciated a small phamplet explaining the techniques with their purchase. It made the piece something special. It somehow suggested to buyers that could purchase an item as a gift for friends and relatives, that pottery made good gifts to take home. The printed information is automatically included with every sale, and from a psychological point of view adds an appearance of generosity on the potter's part. Eventually a two page advertising sheet was developed and printed with all pertinent information and a picture of the potter. The information on these two pages contains the following:

1. Introduction of the artist-potter

2. The type of ware and technique used

3. Description of glazes used in the pottery

The total cost of all advertising expenses, which include advertising in a weekly, local paper, printed matter, and letter heads plus shipping materials have never amounted to more than one or two percent of net income.

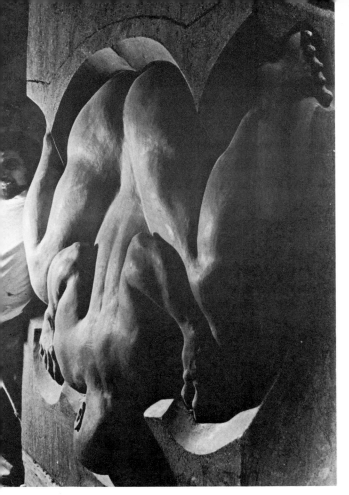

Figure 159. "Big dish in white with ceramic stones in different colors." Stoneware 1970, by Karin Bjorquist, Sweden.

Figure 157. Jerry Rothman, State University of Iowa. Mr. Rothman is acclaimed for his pioneering and building of mammoth clay objects on wooden scaffold systems. His contributions in expanding the traditional limitations of size in clay made objects have made him nationally known and highly respected as a potter and teacher.

Figure 158. William Marshall, England. Salt glazed bowl with slip decoration, 6 inches diameter.

Figure 160. Alfred Saidl, Austria, unglazed torso, slab built, approximate height 42 inches.

Figure 161. "Iron Horse," painted earthenware, 24 x 34 inches, by Steve Andersen, Colorado.

Figure 162. Wheelthrown sculpture, stoneware, by potter Herbert C. Schumacher, University of Northern Colorado.

A POTTER'S DREAM

Thus far the study of the set-up of the Silverton Mountain Pottery has been dealt with from a techno-economical point of view. Recognizing the diversity of circumstances which one faces in any such undertaking, only a few suggestions have been made, all of which should be of considerable aid to any one attempting to establish his own shop. In retrospect, perhaps, the most important test of the Silverton Pottery was of an intrinsic character, the hope that it would provide an answer to the question; how much integrity must an artist craftsman relinquish to be able to produce salable items to the average public. After four years of constant success, the answer is astonishing, it is definitely *none*. If one does not consider oneself a perennial experimenter the potter has nothing to worry about, the argument whether utility to some degree is valid or not simply does not apply. If a person considers himself a sculptor, or painter in clay, which is entirely up to the individual, then the one-man shop idea is not for him. In this great age of diversity arguments concerning the status of the crafts within the framework of the visual arts are at most academic and always pointless. The Silverton idea represents so much more, it provides for the potter not only a place to sell his wares for a just reward, but enables him to pursue some of his philosophies with conviction.

During the course of the past few generations of the machine age all arts have been isolated from the main stream of life and have been forced into ivory towers. In much of the planning of our environment aesthetic considerations have been kept far in the background or left out entirely. Society has succumbed to a conformity imposed upon it by mass production methods which having raised the levels of physical comfort, have also dulled the capacity of the masses for aesthetic perception. As a result of this gap Americans today to a great extent live in an era of perfect tools but confused aims and ideals. Often, to the detriment of democracy, American techniques are admired everywhere, but the American way of life hardly commands unqualified respect in the world. The future may depend upon a badly needed balance between the democratic ideals of individualism and the conformity of mass-production. A vigorous participation of the artistically gifted in the planning of our environment would promote genuine understanding. The artist craftsman, because of a degree of utility in his art, can and should stand at the firing line giving truly aesthetic expression to common desires. His work can spread the message well understood by all people rather than only a selected few individuals. After all, this was the dream shared by Morris, Gropius, Leach, and numerous others who believe in purpose and humanity. Somewhere, sometime, a deliberate attempt will have to be made to bridge the gap between the organization man and the artist in our society for the benefit of all.

In some minute way, over the span of years and summers, the author hopes that the Silverton Mountain Pottery can and will contribute in the building of that bridge, to actively disseminate an understanding of aesthetically high design standards in useful items.

Figure 163. Raku cup from Japan, origins unknown.

Appendix

Techniques, Ideas and Hints

WEDGING CLAY

Thorough wedging of the clay improves its consistency and aids in the removal of minute air bubbles which may have remained in the clay after processing. Any sturdy surface, if covered with a canvas will do for the wedging process. A canvas cover on the *wedging-bat* will prevent the clay from sticking to the surface during the process.

Almost every potter has his favorite way of wedging and believes that his technique is the best one for the purpose. The most common way to wedge is to *knead* the clay in *loaf-size* chunks not unlike the kneading of a loaf of bread, continually cutting the clay in halves during the process and slamming the two halves forcefully into each other. In the Orient a twist with palm of the hand has been added that *kneads* the *clay into a spiral form* which is considered to render the clay more perfect. Whichever way the student may decide to wedge his clay is relatively secondary to the time one spends wedging. A well-wedged clay is absolutely necessary for any success in wheel throwing, and any wedging process should be continued until one feels a smooth, air free, consistence of the clay body.

KERAMOS is for teachers of pottery, it presents here two additional methods of wedging which have proven useful in classroom situations. Both methods are relatively easy to learn, are relatively fast, are noiseless, and prevent the need for great muscle-power.

Figure 164. Kenji Kato, Tajimi Pottery, Japan. Mr. Kato demonstrates wedging the clay the Japanese way during a demonstration in Denver.

Figure 165. Potter Don Reitz wedging a 45 lb. lump of clay.

Figure 166. When chop-wedging the clay is cut into slices, these slices are then chopped down with the side of the hand on top of each other. Chop-wedging is fast, relatively noiseless, and does not require great muscle-power.

Figure 167. Stroke-wedging improves the consistency of clay in a fast and quiet way. The clay slices are evenly distributed on top of each other with rhythmical, strokelike movements using the palm of one's hand.

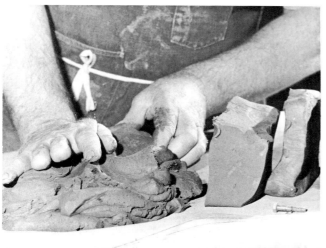

For a lack of a better name they are known as *chop-wedging* and *stroke-wedging*. Stroke-wedging rapidly improves the consistency of any clay. The clay is held with one hand and stroked with the other palm across the wedging-bat. This is repeated several times, then the clay is formed back into a loaf, and the loaf is cut into several one to two-inch slices for *chop-wedging*. Chop-wedging aids in the removal of air bubbles in the clay. The individual slices are placed on top of each other and "chopped" down forcefully. After several "choppings" the clay is ready for use.

FORMING THE CLAY

No matter how sophisticated the tools and how perfect the technique that is used to form clay, the end result is up to the potter and not to the clay he may be using. The properties of clay as a dynamic medium of expression must be understood by the potter, and these must be utilized with restraint and sensitivity. Clay is pliable and will give way to the pressure of one's fingers; but, this in itself is no guarantee that one will press in the right place at the right time. It is a readiness to understand and to experiment, and foremost to spend ample time with the material that will bring success and satisfaction to the student.

Clay can be formed in many ways. Raw ceramic bodies can be cast into *forms* and *molds* and *jiggered* when mass-production is desirable. In today's manufacturing plants sophisticated jiggering machines manufacture hundreds of precisely alike tea cups each hour. It is the hand processes of *wheel throwing, coil* and *slab* building and their combinations that interest the artist-potter and the student most. These processes the artist-potter has always at his disposal no matter how small, or, large his studio may be. The intent of KERAMOS as has been stated before, has never been to be a complete technical manual, such literature is amply available for those interested. Nevertheless, a number of guidelines are presented here for the beginning and intermediate student which may be helpful to him in developing his skills. The professional, or, advanced potter gained his skills through a long apprenticeship, this sometimes marks his products with a *machine-like* character which is seldom a virtue. Very often, pottery produced by prim-

Figure 174. Professor Don Reitz using handles for decorative purposes.

Figure 177. When a foot is desired on a bottle-shape, it must cut into the bottle in its leather hard state with the use of a *clay-chuck*. Clay-chucks can be made from body-clay and used unfired when dry. When they become chipped and old, they can be broken up and new ones made. The author has used such raw chucks for years at a time. Leveling of the pot with a small waterlevel will aid in cutting a level foot.

Figure 175. A sculptural, lidded and handled pot by Ron Meyers, potter at the University of South Carolina.

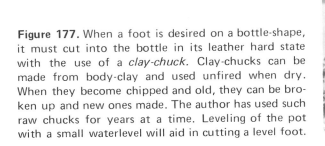

Figure 177-A. Wire loop-tools, plaster carving tools, and individually designed "foot-tools" are readily made. The clay-chucks can also be in a variety of sizes for smaller and larger bottle shapes.

Figure 176. Potter Jim Cantrell throwing in his Bereta, Kentucky, studio.

Figure 178. Bowls and flat shapes are fastened directly to the wheel head using rolled out clay wads.

Figure 179-A. Pots can also be made from coils of clay. The coils can either be rolled out in "nudel" fashion, or they can be cut from rolled out clay slabs with knives and wire-loops.

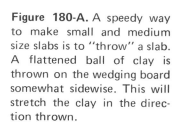

Figure 180-A. A speedy way to make small and medium size slabs is to "throw" a slab. A flattened ball of clay is thrown on the wedging board somewhat sidewise. This will stretch the clay in the direction thrown.

Figure 179-B. The coils are then stacked on top of each other, using slip to attach the coils firmly.

Figure 180-B. By changing the direction in which the clay is "thrown" on top of the wedging board the slab will form the desired shape.

Figure 179-C. The coils must be securely worked into each other to form a solid bond if they are to survive several firings.

Figure 181-A. Slabs of clay are easy with the use of a "slab-board." The board consists of a canvas covered piece of 3/4" plywood upon which two strips of wood have been attached. This allows for a fast construction of large slabs and retards the usual cracking of slabs on the edges when compressed by a rolling pin.

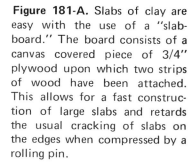

Figure 181-B. A new slab making machine has been designed, and is now produced by Bill Farrell of the Chicago School of Design.

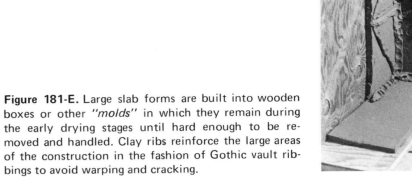

Figure 181-E. Large slab forms are built into wooden boxes or other *"molds"* in which they remain during the early drying stages until hard enough to be removed and handled. Clay ribs reinforce the large areas of the construction in the fashion of Gothic vault ribbings to avoid warping and cracking.

Figure 182. "Sparrows," stoneware plaque by the author.

Figure 181-C. In slab construction cut form from clay slabs are connected with each other by a roughing up of the connecting surface and a generous application of slip. Both sides are then gently pressed together. . . .

Figure 181-D. . . . And strengthened by the addition of a coil of clay which is pressed into the joint.

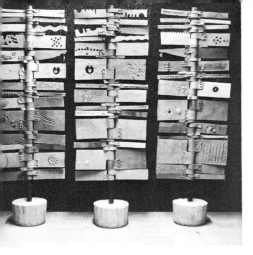

Figure 183. Section of a patio screen from unglazed stoneware slabs, approximately 6 feet high. John Kudlacek, Kansas.

Figure 184. Slab built form by John Schumacker, Colorado.

THE POTTER'S WHEEL

In early books on pottery chapters on potter's wheels were always long and extensive. This was because potter's wheels were hard to obtain. When manufactured by industry for industry, they were heavy, oversized and expensive, out of reach for most artist-potters. Today, fortunately, it is relatively easy to acquire a potter's wheel, CERAMICS MONTHLY and other professional publications are filled with advertisements of wheels of every size, description, and price. Purchased wheels perform satisfactorily most of the time, barring the size of pots one wants to throw, they always work well. For large pots, of course, heavier wheels will do a better job.

Nevertheless, for the more adventuresome student a "make-it-yourself" wheel has been included here. The basic idea for the wheel comes from Paul Soldner, who besides of designing wheels to sell, has also designed crushers, clay mixers, and burners. There is only one advise to give to the student who will attempt to build the wheel, that is: use patience and lots of time to *center* the wheel from the beginning to the end. Every hole, every bearing should be in perfect center.

1. Axel made from 1 1/4 inch black pipe.
2. Floor flange fastens the axel to the throwing head.
3. Throwing head from 3/4 inch exterior plywood.
4. Bearing block made from hardwood, greased when in operation.
5. Concrete flywheel, poured on a ext. plywood form (6).
6. Exterior plywood form for the flywheel.
7. Bottom, ballbearing receptacle mounted to a 2 x 6 or the floor.*
8. Single ball from a ballbearing.
9. Pipe cap functioning as the upper ballbearing receptacle.*

*To hold the single steel ball in place only a *partial hole* of proper size, (depending the size of the ball) is drilled. The single ball will function well as a balanced ballbearing.

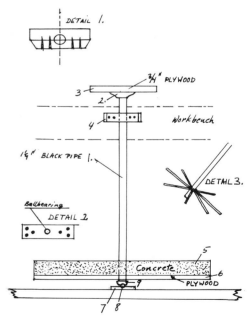

Figure 184-A. Potter's wheel designed by Paul Soldner. The new feature is that it can be assembled from simple standard parts available in any hardware store.

Figure 184-B. A heavy wheel with a **300** pound fly-wheel built by artist-potter Forrest Gist, Belton, Texas. This wheel will take almost any size of clay ball up to sixty and seventy pounds. A half horse power motor gives it strength for throwing large shapes.

Figure 184-C. A standard equipped throwing room at Texas Tech University. The wheels in the front are motorized Paul Soldner kick-wheels.

DECORATING CLAY

The best decoration of clay objects is a well conceived and executed form. Nevertheless, ceramic objects can often be enhanced in many ways provided that the basic form is kept firmly in mind when the decorating technique and application are selected. Any decoration of pottery must affirm rather than deny the basic form of the pot. A form-fitting design can without doubt sophisticate a rather simple form and significantly add to its general beauty.

Basically decorating processes are divided into two basic groups: (1) decorating before firing, and (2) decorating after initial firing. In the first group scraffito, intarsia, carving, and applique make the core with all slip decoration applied on leather-hard clay. In the second group, slip and engobe decor, glazing, under and overglaze painting, and lusters are included. Needless to say, most effective and imaginative potters achieve their best results by combining several of the techniques mentioned. When decorating as in any phase of the craft, only the creative imagination of the artist marks his limit. The tools used for decorating are also of such great array that it would be futile to attempt to mention them individually. Any item that can be used for painting, scratching, stamping, carving, texturing, and modeling is usable. Any advice that may be due should encourage the student to carry out their decorating attempts *with the form in mind.* They should definitely experiment beyond the scope of this presentation to work on their own. It is only when one loses the natural limitations that form imposes upon the artist, that decorations become tortured, super-imposed, incongrous designs, and these are a horror to the true craftsman.

GLAZE AND BODY FORMULAS

Unlimited variations of glazes for any clay body can be derived from the following glaze formulas, even by relative beginners, when the *ten rules for glaze changing* are applied. The important factor to remember for meaningful experimentation is to keep

Figure 185. Master potter Stig Lindberg, Sweden, developing one of his scraffito decorated bottles.

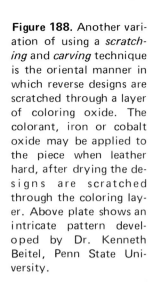

Figure 188. Another variation of using a *scratching* and *carving* technique is the oriental manner in which reverse designs are scratched through a layer of coloring oxide. The colorant, iron or cobalt oxide may be applied to the piece when leather hard, after drying the designs are scratched through the coloring layer. Above plate shows an intricate pattern developed by Dr. Kenneth Beitel, Penn State University.

Figure 186. Somewhat related to stamping is this *Resist Relief*—a technique developed by Roger Corsaw, professor of ceramics at the University of Oklahoma. A design is applied with molten wax on a leather hard pot. After wax hardens, the around the wax design is *washed out,* using a soft, wet sponge. The wax burns out in the bisque firing, preserving the original design.

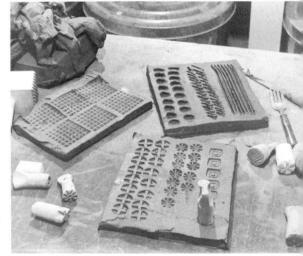

Figure 189. Next to scraffito, stamping is perhaps the most popular method of decoration. Stamps can be made from clay, bisque fired and used for an unlimited time. Many every-day throwaways lend themselves excellently for stamping.

Figure 187. Any tool that can be used to scratch a design into soft clay can be used to decorate by the craffito method, the possibilities of textures and patterns are literally unlimited.

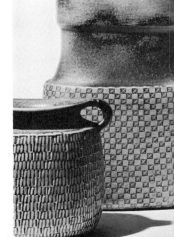

Figure 190. These two stoneware pots have been decorated with an over-all stamped pattern, covered with an iron glaze, the repeated stamping forms a beautiful texture. Stig Lindberg, Sweden.

112

Figure 191. A rich harvest of stamping, applied clay coils, and scraffito decor can be seen in the pots of Richard Peeler from the University of Indiana.

Figure 193-A. A very popular technique is *wax resist*. The technique is simple and can be varied in several ways. From experience, the best emulsion to be used is made from 50% bees wax and 50% stearin, although melted, left-over candle stumps will work just as well. Commercial wax-resist emulsion is inferior and harder to use. The above illustration shows a small, inexpensive enameling (any hot plate will do) being used to melt the wax.

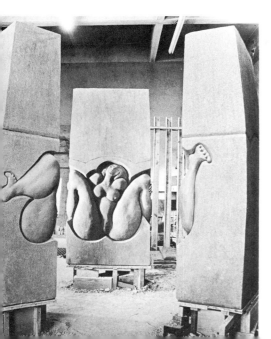

Figure 192. Forms with heavy, thick walls can be *carved* into while the clay is leather hard. Above one of the monumental pieces of master-potter Jerry Rothman, Iowa. The sculpture is 10' tall.

Figure 193-B. The wax can be applied: (1) on raw dry, or bisqued clay, then covered with any coloring agent and glazed. (2) The form can first be colored and then the wax applied, after which it is glazed. (3) Wax resists can also be used on a layer of glaze on the pot, after which another layer of glaze of another color is applied and fired.

Rubber resist is a deviation of wax resist and can be applied in similar situations. The difference between using wax, or liquid rubber latex is that the latter has harder edges and does not produce the typical dropspotting of wax. In rubber resist, the design is painted on the form with liquid rubber latex, or, (rubber cement) after drying and then glazing the stretchy rubber layer is pulled off.

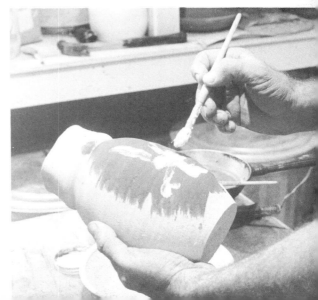

Figure 194. Wax resist decorated bottle by potter Clyde Burt, Melrose, Ohio. Stoneware, 29 inches high.

Figure 195. The above vase with wax resist iron pigment decoration by the English potter William Marshall is a fine example of the technique.

Figure 196. A good example of underglaze painting is this large, lidded jar by master-potter James McKinnell, Colorado. Mr. McKinnell and his wife Nan are acknowledged as two of the best craftsmen in this country.

Figure 197. Underglaze painting with coloring oxides, stains, and engobes knows no limits to the imagination. Sheldon Carrey, Kansas, used iron oxide, painted on the bisqued pots covered by a flowing glaze, the effects are stunning.

Figure 198. With the advent of new commercial techniques of making reproductions, many of them find their way into ceramics. Victor Spinski, Delaware has developed some fascinating results with silk-screen images on ceramic surfaces. He scrupulously follows the commercial techniques in developing his screens, and uses low fusing, commercial stains mixed with a mild gum solution as printing medium. The addition of a "pinch" of ball clay to the mixed stain assures a clearer image later. Once the image is applied to the pot, the whole is fired to the maturing temperature of the stain. The most important thing is to avoid over-firing as this tends to "fuse the image" and obstruct its clarity. Photo stencils can be obtained by interested potters from commercial, silk-screening establishments. Commercial ceramic stains serve as the printing medium.

Figure 199. Photo images can also be readily transferred to ceramic surfaces. Photo-sensitive emulsions are available to the potter with detailed instructions from the ROCKLAND COLLOID CORPORATION, Piermont, New York, 10968. To produce a photo image the pot is treated like any photograph, that is exposed, developed and fixed. The potter needs an enlarger and dark room facilities for the process. Above the author shows a large slab construction with photo image.

Figure 201-A. Glazes can be painted on with a brush, they can be sprayed on with a paint sprayer, poured and dipped. All these processes can be used singly, applying one "only" glaze coat on a pot, or, as is usual with artists who desire their pieces to be unique works of art, they can be used combined. A pot can be sprayed with one glaze first and another glaze painted on immediately after the first one sets. Another potter may prefer to paint iron oxide on first, then dip the pot in one glaze, and later pour a third glaze on top of it. The most popular method with the artist-potter and student, and the one best suited for personal expression is pouring, or dipping the glazes. This illustration shows a glaze being poured into a bisque fired object. The glaze coat should be approximately a 1/32 to 1/8 inch thick. Many excellent effects can be achieved by dipping and pouring glazes of different colors and textures on top of each other.

Figure 200. The whole array of possibilities and potential glaze applications, of overlapping glazes of different colors, different firing temperatures, different degrees of viscosity come to mind in the details of a pot by one of America's young but significant potters. The detail shows the use of low fire lusters over a finished stoneware glaze, by Les Lawrence, Arizona. Many of the effects of ancient potters on all continents were achieved by such combinations and *double-applications.*

Figure 201-B. Large shapes and open bowls can best be poured by placing them on supporting strips of wood over large containers, and then pouring the glaze over them. This method saves glazes as the surplus can be poured back into the glaze batch without harm. Dipping and pouring are also the safest, and fastest methods for the artist-potter. No special equipment is necessary and no dangerous dust affects the breathing.

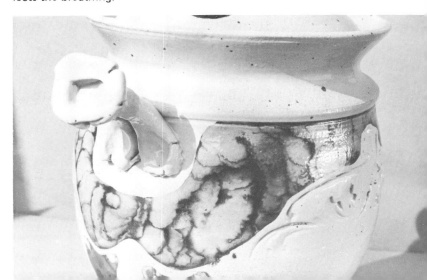

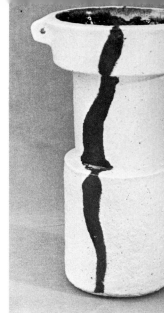

Figure 201-C. A bottle shape being dipped into a large container of well-stirred glaze. See the chapter on glazes for best consistency. A thin coat of wax applied to the bottom of pots will make the *crow-footing* (dry-footing) later on much easier.

Figure 203. Porcelain vase, 12 inches, slab construction by Janet Leach, England. Celadon glaze, black glaze decor, reduction firing.

Figure 202. Glazes can also be painted on with brushes, sponged on, spattered on, and applied by any means the potter can think of. Don Reitz, Wisconsin.

Figure 204. Large wall mural, unglazed clay with slip decoration, 4 x 8 feet, potter Paul Hatgil, University of Texas.

replacing *flux for flux,* and *clays for clays,* and to raise or lower the flint (silica) content to affect maturing temperatures.

Any feldspatic glaze can be converted into a wood ash glaze with pleasing effects, when the feldspar in the glaze is gradually replaced with wood ashes on a percentual basis. A line test were 10% of wood ashes replace 10% of feldspar successively will produce good results.

All glazes presented here are basic glaze formulas which can be opacified or colored by the use of standard coloring agents. (See chapter on glazes.) Triangle blends on the same glaze with a different stain or coloring oxide on the three corners will produce many pleasing and exciting textures and hues.

Also, many unusual hues and textures can be achieved by a meaningful replacement of the ball clays and kaolins in the formulas with local clays or the body clay. The same percentage procedure as mentioned for ash replacement is to follow.

Regarding the clay-body formulas; many clays can be used as found in nature when processed accordingly. Nevertheless, it is more useful to the artist-potter to have a well prepared, reliable ceramic body to work with. Its consistency in terms of chemical composition often decides how glazes and other effects of color and textures can be produced. The following ceramic bodies are to be considered starting points for meaningful experimentation for the student. By exchanging local clays for kaolins and ball clays, and adding grogs and other aggregates, numerous well-balanced and indivudualized clay bodies can be derived.

Figure 205. Ready for a sale day. A view of the pottery of the Austin artist-potter Ishmael Soto. Mr. Soto uses only local materials in his work and is widely acclaimed throughout the Southwest.

Figure 206. Potter Ishmael Soto closing his kiln. Soto designed and built the kiln including the burner system.

GLAZE FORMULAS

The following glaze formulas are based on *parts-by-weight* and can be used for small test batches (using grams) or larger batches using ounces or pounds.

LOW FIRE GLAZES:

WHITE MAJOLICA GLAZE   CONE 015

Leadfrit	380
White lead	280
Lithium carbonate	80
Flint	190
Tin oxide	90
1% Bentonite	

CLEAR GLAZE   CONE 015

WHITE LEAD	300
FRIT (leadless)	300
Lithium carbonate	80
Flint	280
1% Bentonite	

CLEAR LEADLESS GLAZE   CONE 015

BOROSILICATE FRIT	650
Lithium carbonate	100
Flint	190
1% Bentonite	

TRANSPARENT GLAZE   CONE 04

Any lead frit	500
Nepheline Syenite	152
Ball clay	126
Whiting	55
Flint	167

CONE 04 MATTE GLAZE   CONE 04

White lead	354
Whiting	60
Feldspar, potash	190
Barium carbonate	130
Zinc oxide	38
Kaolin	70
Flint	180

CLEAR, GLOSSY GLAZE   CONE 04

WHITE LEAD	100
Borax	100
Flint	160

FLOWING OPAQUE GLAZE   CONE 04

White lead	521
Feldspar	91
Flint	115
Borax	76
Whiting	58
Tin oxide	50

LOW FIRE SLIP GLAZE   CONE 04

Medium to dark brown color

White lead	600
Red brick clay	400

LOW FIRE SLIP GLAZE   CONE 04
Ceramics Monthly, Oct., 1965

This glaze is suitable as under-glaze for oil spot effects.

Barnard clay	500
Red lead	500

WHITE GLOSS GLAZE   CONE 04
Ceramics Monthly, Oct., 1965

When this glaze is thickly applied over the above slip glaze, and is slightly over fired, beautiful oil spot effects can result.

Ferro frit 3134	193
Ferro frit 3304	417
Zircopax	266
Ball clay	124

SWEDISH SLIP GLAZE

Red lead	1000
Natural brick clay	550
or:	
Red lead	1000
Kaolin	330

EARTHENWARE GLAZE USED
IN DENMARK

Feldspar (Kona 4)	834
Whiting	150
White lead	160
Kaolin	516

WHITE EARTHENWARE GLAZE

FELDSPAR	556
White lead	206
Flint	54
Tin oxide	27

WHITE EARTHENWARE GLAZE

Feldspar	556
Whiting	200
Red lead	1603
Flint	660
Tin oxide	300

BARIUM-ZINC MATTE GLAZE

Feldspar	380
Whiting	40
White lead	406
Barium carbonate	130
Zinc oxide	32
Kaolin	70
Potters flint	150

CONE 04-02

CONE 04

This glaze is somewhat opaque and useful with many coloring agents.

This glaze is easily opacified with 8% Tin oxide and accepts all standard coloring agents.

CONE 04-02

CONE 04-02

CONE 04

LOW FIRE IRRIDESCENT GLAZE,
Irene Kettner

Lead-borosilicate frit (Pemco PB 461)	746
Red iron oxide	224
Royal blue underglaze	30

AKATSUKA RAW URANIUM RED-
ORANGE, R. Schneider

White lead	350
Potters flint	100
Uranium oxide	80

RICH RED URANIUM GLAZE,
Bezanson

Feldspar	92
White lead	850
Zinc oxide	8
Potters flint	50
Uranium oxide	200

BRIGHT RED URANIUM GLAZE

White lead	666
Nepheline syenite	168
Zinc oxide	32
Potters flint	170

VOLCANIC ASH GLAZE, Carrey

Volcanic ash	700
Colmanite	300
Bentonite	50

VOLCANIC ASH GLAZE, Carrey

Eagle pitcher lead silicate	314
LV-1 volcanic ash	250

CONE 04

Sift dry materials through 80 mesh screen, mix to creamy consistency, apply thickly by building up several thin layers.

CONE 011

Red-orange transparent glaze, Strict oxidation.

CONE 04

Matte, opaque, rich red-orange with occasional black splotches. Strict oxidation.

CONE 04

Strict oxidation.

22% black uranium oxide.

CONE 04-10

CONE 02-1

(handwritten, top right: potters flint Lepidolite)

Keystone feldspar	28
Colmanite	55
Whiting	21
Zinc oxide	32
Barium carbonate	42
O-38-4 clay	85
Potters flint	52
Zircopax	121

Produces a good shade of yellow with 5% commercial stain.

VOLCANIC ASH GLAZE, Carrey — CONE 7-9

Volcanic ash	399
Whiting	84
Magnesium carbonate	73
Barium carbonate	49
Ball clay	285
Potters flint	100

Colored glazes can be made by adding glaze stains or standard coloring oxides.

COLORLESS MATTE GLAZE — CONE 5-6

Feldspar	560
Whiting	500
White lead	1030
Ball clay	1030

ALBANY SLIP GLAZE — CONE 5-6

(handwritten: 9 6 dry)

Albany slip	272
Red iron oxide	46
Nepheline syenite	180
Kaolin	20
Borax	20

"A" MATTE GLAZE, Carlton Ball — CONE 5-6

Feldspar	332
White lead	150
Dolomite	107
Whiting	59
Kaolin	147
Albany slip	140
Flint	50

For speckles add 15 parts granular manganese.

CRATERED GLAZE, Richard Behrens — CONE 6

Ceramic talc	455
Lepidolite *(handwritten ? mark)*	544
Bentonite	20

MATTE PATTERNED GLAZE, Richard Behrens — CONE 6

Lepidolite *(handwritten ? mark)*	503
Whiting	199
Potters flint	298
Bentonite	20

CLEAR GLAZE CONE 5, Penn. State — CONE 5

(handwritten: 8 6 dry)

Ball clay	500
Colemanite	500

ROSS MATTE, Penn. State — CONE 2-4

Oxidation or reduction firing.

Feldspar	800
Whiting	120
Barium carbonate	150
Zinc oxide	120
Talc	40
Kaolin	100
Ball clay	80
Potters flint	360

ALKALINE MATTE GLAZE, Penn. State — CONE 5

Nepheline syenite	500
Barium carbonate	100
Lithium carbonate	50
Frit 3110	50
Whiting	50
Potters flint	150
Kaolin	100

JACK HOPKINS GLAZE

White lead	1200
Whiting	250
Zinc oxide	
Calcined ball clay	380
Potters flint	870

CELADON GLAZE, Carlton Ball

Kingman feldspar	262
Whiting	52
Zinc oxide	8
Kaolin	47
Potters flint	59
Red iron oxide	8

GLOSSY BRISTOL GLAZE

Feldspar	600
Potters flint	150
Whiting	120
Zinc oxide	60
Ball clay	100

ZINC-BARIUM GLAZE

Feldspar	580
Whiting	42
Zinc oxide	70
Barium carbonate	52
Ball clay	67
Potters flint	180

MATTE ZINC-BARIUM GLAZE

Feldspar	541
Whiting	117
Zinc oxide	64
Barium carbonate	61
Magnesium carbonate	21
Ball clay	140
Potters flint	60

CONE 5

4% Tin oxide and 5% black iron oxide produce a medium, opaque brown.

CONE 5-6

CONE 5-7

CONE 6

Good for Blues

CONE 6

BASIC MATTE CALCIUM GLAZE — CONE 5-7

Feldspar	478
Whiting	124
Zinc oxide	65
Barium carbonate	56
Magnesium carbonate	16
Ball clay	265

LOW FIRE WOOD ASH GLAZE, MATTE — CONE 04-02

White lead	457
Potash feldspar	276
Ball clay	121
Calcined clay	14
Mixed wood ashes	132

LOW FIRE WOOD ASH GLAZE — CONE 04

White lead	300
Feldspar	160
Ball clay	36
Kaolin	48
Mixed wood ash (unwashed)	60

LOW FIRE WOOD ASH GLAZE, H. L. Thurn — CONE 04-02

White lead	439
Feldspar	278
Ball clay	121
Calcined clay	28
Wood ash	134

MEDIUM FIRE WOOD ASH GLAZE — CONE 5-6

FELDSPAR	400
Medium wood ash	400
Ball clay (any)	200

ASH GLAZE   CONE 8

Feldspar	350
Wood ash	350
Ball clay	300

ASH GLAZE, BUTTERY TEXTURE   CONE 8-9

Feldspar	350
Wood ash	350
Ball clay	300
Dolomite	38
Potters flint	30

ASH GLAZE   CONE 9-10

Mixed unwashed ash	350
Feldspar	350
Kaolin	150
Talc	150

The ash was sieved twice through a sixty mesh sieve.

ASH GLAZE   CONE 9-10

Mixed ash, unwashed	200
Feldspar	350
Dolomite	150
Kaolin	100
Potters flint	200

This glaze displayed best results with 3% rutile, and 2% iron oxide as coloring agents.

ASH GLAZE   CONE 9-10

Mixed ash	300
Ball clay	300
Feldspar	300

BROWN ASH GLAZE   CONE 9-10

Mixed ash	300
Ball clay	250
Albany slip	50
Feldspar	300
Red iron oxide	18

PLUM COLORED GLAZE   CONE 9-10

Cornwall stone	250
Albany slip	550
Red iron oxide	110
Whiting	100

MASON'S RED GLAZE   CONE 9-10

Potash Feldspar	400
Bone ash	112
Dolomite	62
Red iron oxide	50
Ball clay	37
Potters flint	50

SEMI-MATTE, Nelson   CONE 8-10

Feldspar	664
Whiting	80
Kaolin	256

SEMI-GLOSS BLACK GLAZE,   CONE 8-10
Nelson

| Albany slip clay | 1000 |
| Cobalt oxide | 50 |

COPPER BLUE GLAZE,   CONE 9-10
Carlton Ball

Nepheline syenite	437
Barium carbonate	343
Ball clay	63
Rutile	88

4% cooper carbonate

COPPER BLUE GLAZE,   CONE 10
Silverton Mt. Pottery

Nepheline syenite	526
Barium carbonate	315
Lithium carbonate	20
Potters flint	80
Copper carbonate	30

COPPER RED GLAZE, Spinski — CONE 9-10

Potash feldspar	360
Whiting	22.5
Colmanite	75
Dolomite	75
Zinc oxide	15
Barium carbonate	37.5
Kaolin	42.5
Potters flint	225
Tin oxide	22.5
Copper carbonate	4

Apply by double dipping, layers will form different hues of red to copper blue.

COPPER RED — CONE 9-10

Potash feldspar	300
Dolomite	150
Colmanite	120
Barium carbonate	80
Kaolin	50
Potters flint	320
Tin oxide	20
Copper carbonate	8
Silican carbide	8

COPPER RED, Glen Nelson, *Ceramics* — CONE 9-10

Ferro frit 3191	130
Feldspar (soda)	440
Whiting	140
Kaolin	30
Potters flint	250
Tin oxide	10
Copper carbonate	2

This glaze has been used at the Silverton pottery with a slight adjustment; (1) any boro-silicate frit at hand has been used, and (2) any kaolin will work successfully. The glaze requires a medium reduction for the last 4 cones during high altitude firing.

Especially beautiful reds have been achieved when this glaze is applied over a standard copper blue glaze.

BLUE CELADON GLAZE, Lakofsky — CONE 9-10

Feldspar	213
Dalton Clay	14
Whiting	67
Dolomite	250
Potters flint	180
Iron oxide	5
Tin oxide	10

Any slip clay will work for Dalton Clay.

BRANNAN BLUE SHING GLAZE — CONE 9-10

Feldspar	800
Whiting	300
Kaolin	200
Potters flint	500
Talc	200

G-9 WAXY MATTE, Spinski — CONE 9-10

Feldspar	560
Barium carbonate	190
Whiting	70
Zinc oxide	70
Ball clay	90
Rutile	20

Used successfully at the University of Delaware in the classes of Mr. Victor Spinski

G-3 LIGHT GREEN — CONE 9-10

Feldspar	510
Barium carbonate	210
Whiting	80
Zinc oxide	80
Rutile	20
Copper carbonate	16

Used successfully at the University of Delaware in the classes of Mr. Victor Spinski

WHITE ZIRCONIUM GLAZE — CONE 8-10

Potash feldspar	351
Whiting	135
Zinc oxide	20
Ball clay	100
Zircopax	234
Potters flint	150

Smooth, bright, white glaze should serve well for colored glazes.

HARD PORCELAIN GLAZE — CONE 9-10

Potash feldspar	421
Whiting	186
Ball clay	131
Potters flint	242

DRISCOLL STONEWARE GLAZE — CONE 9-10

Feldspar	200
Whiting	150
Body stoneware clay	250
Red iron oxide	150
Potters flint	250

TRANSPARENT BASE GLAZE, Bernard Leach, *A Potters Book* — CONE 8-10

Feldspar	400
Whiting	200
Kaolin	100
Potters flint	300

BASIC LEADLESS RAKU GLAZE, Paul Soldner — CONE 012-09

Gerstley borate	50
Powdered borax	50

BASIC LEAD RAKU GLAZE, Bernard Leach — CONE 012-09

White lead	60
Lead frit	20
Potters flint	20

BASIC WHITE RAKU GLAZE — CONE 012-09

White lead	70
Lead frit	20
Potters flint	10
Tin oxide	10

SOLDNER CLEAR RAKU GLAZE, Paul Soldner — CONE 012-09

Gerstley borate	70
Plastic Vitrox (P.V. clay)	30

GLASS RED RAKU, Paul Soldner — CONE 012-09

Gerstley borate	30
Borax	50
Red Iron oxide	10
Copper oxide	5

CURDLE BLUE, Paul Soldner — CONE 012-09

Gerstley borate	50
Borax	50
Cobalt oxide	0.5
Rutile	3

1/2/3/ WAXY MATTE, Paul Soldner — CONE 012-09

Gerstley borate	30
Kaolin	20
Potters flint	10

TRANSPARENT THICK RAKU — CONE 012-09

Glass cullet	20
White lead	110
Potters flint	20

RAKU; LOCAL CLAY BODY

Local brick clay	500
Medium grog	500
Body bentonite	20

RAKU; SOLDNER BODY, Paul Soldner,
Aspen, Colorado

Plastic Fire clay	500
Talc	200
Fine sand (mostly 30 mesh)	300
Water 20%	

RAKU; VARIATION OF SOLDNER'S
CLAY BODY

Fire clay (any)	300
Ball clay	200
Talc	200
Grog	300

CONE 2 LIGHT RED BODY,
Glen Nelson, *Ceramics*

Red clay	600
Potters flint	250
Kaolin	150

EARTHENWARE, TERRA COTTA BODY   CONE 06-2

Local, red brick clay	700
Fire clay (any)	300
Grog 10%	

MEDIUM FIRING RANGE,   CONE 5-8
STONEWARE BODY

Fire clay (any)	100
Red brick clay	100
Ball clay	100
Grog 10 to 15%	

CONE 5-11 STONEWARE BODY,
SAN MARCOS MIX

Plastic Fire clay	100
Red clay	50
Ball clay	20
Plastic Vitrox	30
Grog 12%	

CONE 10 STONEWARE BODY

Fire clay	100
Red clay	50
Ball clay	80
Grog	32

CONE 10 STONEWARE BODY

Fire clay	400
Ball clay	250
Red clay	100
Potters flint	100
Feldspar	100
Grog 10 to 15%	

STONEWARE SCULPTURE BODY

Fire clay	800
Grog (medium and coarse)	200
Red Iron oxide	50

STONEWARE SCULPTURE BODY FOR
LARGE PIECES

Fire clay	700
Grog (medium and coarse	200
Perlite or vermiculite	100
Iron oxide	50

For dark brown, blackish
color, add 2% cobalt oxide.

PORCELAIN THROWING BODY   CONE 8-10

Kaolin	300
Ball clay	250
Feldspar	200
Potters flint	200
Bentonite	25

CONE 8 STONEWARE BODY

Monmouth stoneware clay   100

Fire clay (A.P.Green)   50

Potters flint   50

Grog 5 to 10%

CONE 8 to 10 STONEWARE BODY

Monmouth stoneware clay   100

Kaolin   50

Potters flint   50

Ball clay   50

Fine grog   25

Red Iron oxide   25

This is a red brown body which has been successfully used to throw miniature forms on the potters-wheel.

CONE 8-10 STONEWARE BODY

Stoneware clay   100

Fire clay   100

Red clay   50

Grog 5 to 10%

Jordan or Monmouth will work

CONE 9-10 PORCELAIN BODY

Kaolin   500

Ball clay   150

Feldspar   250

Potters flint   100

JAPANESE PORCELAIN BODY FOR THROWING ON THE WHEEL.

Kaolin (Putnam)   500

Feldspar   375

Potters flint   125

This body was given to me by Dr. Kenneth Beitel from Penn State. The body must be hand-mixed with 50% water and whipped like cream, after which the body is dried-out in a canvas lined box in normal air. The body has excellent throwing qualities.

TABLE OF TEMPERATURE EQUIVALENTS OF STANDARD PYROMETRIC CONES (ORTON).

Cones should be set at a 8° angle for accurate temperature indication.

color	cone #	Fahrenheit	Centigrade
very dull red	022	1121	605
	021	1139	615
	020	1202	650
	019	1220	660
dull red	018	1328	720
	017	1418	770
	016	1463	795
	015	1481	805
	014	1526	830
	013	1580	860
cherry red	012	1607	875
	011	1643	895
	010	1661	905
orange	09	1706	930
	08	1742	950
	07	1814	990
yellow	06	1859	1015
	05	1904	1040
	04	1940	1060
	03	2039	1115
	02	2057	1125
	01	2093	1145
bright yellow	1	2120	1160
	2	2129	1165
	3	2138	1170
	4	2174	1190
	5	2201	1205
	6	2246	1230
yellow white	7	2282	1250
	8	2300	1260
	9	2345	1285
	10	2381	1301
	11	2417	1325
white	12	2435	1335
	13	2462	1350
	14	2552	1400

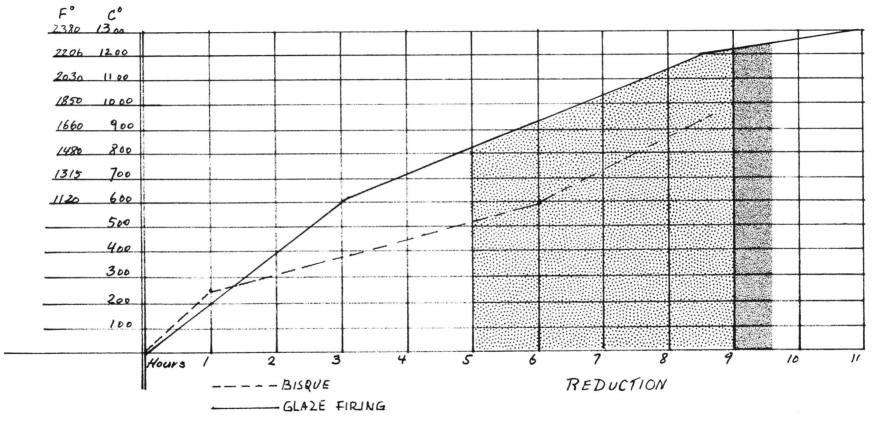

Figure 207. *A chart of ideal firing cycles for glaze and bisque firing.*

A chart as the one above constitutes the kiln-log at the Silverton Mountain Pottery. The firing is plotted each hour and visualizes the progression of tempera-ture for reduction purposes. Kiln results, and remarks are entered on the backside and preserved for later study. The ideal temperature in glaze firing should progress according to a steadily raising line, the degree increase slowing down progressively as the temperature increases. For a bisque fire, the first two hundred degrees can be reached fast, then a very slow period of rising temperature is to be maintained until 600°C., when the core-water in the clay is burned out, after that a speedy finish is most economical.

FIRING CHARTS AND HINTS

For a long time it has been generally accepted that slow out-drawn firing cycles will improve the final appearance of the glaze. In our modern times, of finely ground and purified chemicals, this statement is only partially true. In the past, when most glazes were composed from relatively coarse materials, a long firing cycle may have been important. Gases are formed in the *glaze-melt* by the chemical disassociation of varied material in the batch. These rise to the surface of the melting, honey-like substance, as tiny, microscopic bubbles. This bubbling of the glaze performs a very important mixing action of the melt, which results in a smoother glaze texture. Since science has delivered to the potter materials of high purity and fine grind, and these in turn mix more readily during the melting of the batch, unusually, prolongated firing cycles can be eliminated.

A great majority of potters agree that in a studio situation firing cycles from 8 to 12 hours are desirable and yield satisfactory results. More important than the duration of the firing cycle is the *cooling* of the kiln. When cooling happens slowly, the kiln and the glazes will benefit. The slow cooling off allows gases to escape from the glaze-melt before the glaze sets into its solid state, and slow cooling also aids the formation of micro-crystalline structures within the glaze, the effects of which are every potter's desire.

A general rule of thumb: the cooling off period should be at least twice the time it takes to fire the kiln up.

If possible every kiln should be equipped with a *pyrometer,* a high temperature indicator. Such instruments can now be purchased from ceramic dealers for under $50.00 complete. A pyrometer allows one to follow the rise of the temperature in the kiln but only measures the dry heat, and does not indicate accurately what is happening to the glaze in the kiln. For successful reduction firing it is a must because it allows for a meaningful spacing of "reducing" periods throughout the firing cycle. Pyrometers should therefore, always be used in combination with *pyrometric cones.* The cones are little, slender pyramids composed of specially calculated clay mixes, each calibrated to bend at a certain temperature. They are placed in the kiln, held in place by a small paddy of clay,

and should be visible through the *peep-hole.* While pyrometers indicate the heat, cones will show what is happening to the glaze in terms of the melting process. When working with very heat-sensitive glazes, an even better indicator exists in *draw-trials.*

Figure 208. Pyrometric cones indicate what is happening to the glaze in the kiln.

Draw-trials are made from the same clay as the pot and dipped into the same glaze, and they are placed on a small platform, reachable through an enlarged "peep-hole" from the outside with the aid of a long steel rod. Several can be lined-up and drawn from the kiln at several intervals. Then the trial is cooled off rapidly, and when the glaze appears properly melted the kiln is shut off.

During a glaze firing the pieces in the kiln should be separated from each other not less than ¼ inch. As glazes melt they form a thick, liquid coating which later hardens; pieces touching in the kiln during this time will stick together permanently. During a *bisque firing* pieces can be stacked on top of each other, touch and small pieces put into larger ones for better kiln economy.

Shelves in the kiln should always be covered by *kiln-wash* on their top side. When kiln-wash is applied on the bottom side of the shelves, small bits of wash may contaminate bowls and pot during the glaze firing. An excellent kiln-wash can be made from equal parts of *Flint, Kaolin,* and *coarse Grog.* The grog lends the kiln-wash a rough texture which acts like miniature stilts. This formula can be used at any firing level up to cone 12.

When firing an electric kiln *water-smoking* the kiln for at least one hour is important to avoid water damage to kiln and glazes. In gas and oil fired kilns the water vapors escape through the flue channels and therefore, the kiln-doors and holes can be closed from the beginning.

A simple test whether or not a raw piece is ready for firing is to hold it against one's cheek, should the piece feel cool, then moisture is still present and a danger of cracking exists.

Many glaze defects are due to freshly glazed pots being placed into the kiln. A too fast drying-off of the moisture will cause the glaze cover to peel and form cracks which may crawl later.

Most warping can be avoided when kiln floors are checked periodically to be level, shelves and floors can be propped up with small wads of body-clay to form a perfectly level surface.

When bottoms of vessels are to be glazed they must set on *stilts* for the glaze firing.

Figure 209. Kenji Kato from the Tamimi Pottery, Japan, pulling a *draw-trial.*

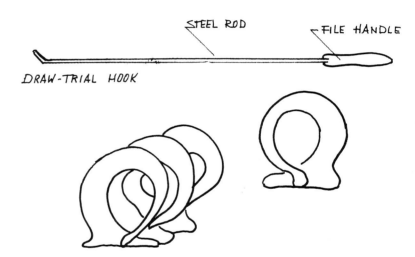

Figure 210. Draw-trials are an inexpensive and accurate heat indicator.

In gas fired kilns, burner pilots can be kept burning overnight to allow thorough drying and avoid cracking later during a fast fire.

Uneven heat in the kiln chamber also will cause warping. Baffle in kilns should always be adjustable and set without mortars. By *tuning* the kiln over a period of several firings a relatively even firing temperature on top and bottom of the kiln should be possible. Stoneware pots are usually *crow-footed* (dry-footed) before placement in the kiln for glaze firing. Crow-footing implies a careful removal of spilled glaze from the vessel's "foot." This cleaning of the bottoms of pots will prevent their sticking to shelves and floor when glaze fired.

Most crystalline glazes require a very slow cooling off period to develop any visible crystallization. The heating-up schedule should be as normal as possible, but a prolonged cooling is recommended. In electric kilns the power can be cut after the last cone bend, but not turned off completely, and gas kiln burners can be turned down too. Each particular glaze combination requires its own particular firing and cooling schedule which will promote maximum crystallization.

Crystalline glazes are very fluid. To prevent damage to the kiln, small clay trays may be made from clay and bisqued, when glaze firing each pot is set upon a *stilt* which is then placed *into the tray*. This effort is very worthwhile as it saves later disappointments concerning chipped and broken pots.

Lead glazes will commonly suffer in a reducing atmosphere, they often appear bubbly and blistered even in slight reduction.

Soaking a kiln at the maturing temperature for 15 to 30 minutes, (depending on the size of the kiln), tends to even out temperature differences in the kiln chamber and benefits most glazes.

When firing a *wood* firing kiln the firing cycle can be sped up after the walls of the chamber become red hot, the fuel can be fed directly into the kiln chamber through openings planned for this purpose. Small pieces of anthracite coal will also speed up a wood firing.

Salt glazing. The best salt glazing results have been achieved at temperatures from cone 8 to cone 11. If salt glazing is desired below cone 7, it becomes necessary to mix borax with the usually used rock salt. Color in salt glazing can be achieved by adding small quantities of coloring oxides to the clay body. Swedish potters repeatedly made use of metal sulfites and sulfates which they paint on the dry but raw pot.

Commonly *rock-salt* which has been premoistened is used, for flashing effects a small quantity of zinc oxide can be experimented with.

Kenneth Ferguson, of the Kansas City Art Institute recommends that "salting holes" should be planned in any salt kiln directly above the fire holes. In this way, as the salt mixture is slowly poured into the kiln chamber, the salt particles slowly float to the bottom, into the fire hole (the hottest part of the kiln), and literally explode into salt vapors.

Figure 211. Manufactured *Stilts* as they can be purchased in many sizes from ceramics dealers.

Figure 212. A set of Raku-tongs made from a standard brake-tool.

Salt glazing yields best results when fired in a reducing atmosphere to allow the development of full, and rich body colors.

Salt glazing kilns should always be of the down-draft type.

European potters often give a new salt kiln a thin wash of pure silica on the inside, and it is common to use extra time and extra amounts of salt for the first few firings until the kiln has been properly "salted".

When the salting begins, the damper should be closed as much as possible without heat loss, the moist rock salt is then "spoon-fed" into the kiln through the salting holes at regular intervals from 5 to 15 minutes, depending upon the condition and size of the kiln.

The thickness and texture of the glaze are best gauged by draw-trials, which are pulled successively before the kiln is shut down for cooling. Bodies with a high silica content are considered best for salt glazing.

Reduction Firing. Many colors and textures develop more subtly and produce mottling effects when matured in a reducing atmosphere. Celadons and copper reds can only be achieved in a reducing atmosphere. Reduction can be achieved in several means: (1) the normal, oxidizing draft is cut down by damper operation, (2) excess fuel is introduced by turning on the gas or oil, (3) local reduction can often be achieved in electric kilns by the addition of silicon carbide to the glaze batch, or the introduction of wood chips and moth balls into the kiln.

When the draft is cut back and more gas is put into a kiln, an incomplete, carbon producing combustion is the result, (in smaller kilns smoke and flames may be visible on top of the stack). Carbon has a great natural affinity for oxygen and will absorb it from the ceramic compounds in the glaze coat, this chemical reaction is commonly known as *reduction*. When through this process of reduction either iron, or copper becomes deprived of an ample supply of oxygen, then they remain suspended in the glaze as particles of pure colloidal metal. Copper tends to produce a beautiful red with occasional blue or purple areas, and iron turns into an olive, or jade-like green.

The addition of minute quantities of *silicon carbide* powder will produce reduction effects in an electric kiln without damage to the kiln. Silicon carbide introduced into any reduction glaze will aid the start of the reduction process. At the Silverton Mountain Pottery a 1/2% of 200 mesh silicon carbide is added to every glaze.

When heavy reduction is started too early, before red heat is apparent in the kiln, glazes may come out dark and unsightly because of trapped carbon particles in the glaze. Reduction should always start after good cherry red heat develops, it should be continued until the warning cone bends, then a short, oxidizing finish of the firing will benefit most glazes.

Most glaze colors require only a neutral, or lightly reducing atmosphere to develop their best properties. Heavy reduction is seldom required and often damaging.

Some glazes benefit by alternating oxidizing and reducing periods during the firing cycle. Only experimentation will indicate which firing schedule is best for a particular glaze.

If reduction is difficult to achieve, dirty oil, discarded from car engines, can be dripped into a kiln using a steel pipe. This will produce a heavy, smokey reduction.

Raku Firing. A good pair of raku-tongs can be made from a standard *brake-tool* available in auto-supply dealers. 3/8" black pipe can be used to lengthen the handles for safe distance.

Raku is commonly fired without cones, by eye-sight, for the beginner a draw-trial can be helpful as most disappointments are the result of too early drawn glazes. A glaze may look shiny and finished in the hot chamber, only to look dull and lifeless when removed from the kiln.

Raku is the most experimental and creative form of pottery firing, experience and persistence are the best teachers. Safety precautions should be observed at all times.

Figure 213. Students having a "raku experience" using a simple stacking kiln, kilnshelves form the "lid," and a "Soldner burner" as illustrated in the kiln section.

Figure 214. Clay forms in the snow, by John Kudlacek.

Glossary

Absorbtion. The soaking up of water by the clay body.

Alkali. A strong chemical base neutralizing acids. Sodium, potassium, calcium, and magnesia.

Alumina. Aluminum oxide.

Ball clay. The most plastic of natural clays. Incredient in most white clay bodies, adds alumina and silica to the body.

Batch. The mixture of weighted ingredients for a quantity of glaze or clay body.

Bentonite. An extremely plastic clay that is added to glazes to improve their suspension factor, and to clay bodies to improve their plasticity.

Bisque. Fired, but unglazed clay items.

Binder. Adhesive, glue, various natural adhesives added to the glaze slip to increase glaze adherence to the bisque fired clay.

Casting. The process of reproducing clay objects in plaster molds/using slip (liquid) clay.

Celadon. The gray and blue-green color in glazes resulting from a reducing atmosphere during the firing.

China. A loosely used term for the general group of vitreous whiteware.

China clay. Kaolin.

Clay. Finely ground earth matter, basically decomposed granite rock, plastic when moist and regaining strength when fired.

Coefficient of Expansion. The rate of change of length of clay with change in temperature.

Coil method. A hand building process of making pottery using clay coils.

Cone, pyrometric. Triangular clay cones, indicators of kiln temperature during the firing.

Crackle glaze. A glaze displaying spider web patterns of minute cracks, when rubbed with coloring oxides and refired at lower temperatures unique decorative effects are achieved.

Crawling. Glaze defect, because of several reasons possible, the glaze crawls up into pools leaving bare clay in between.

Craze. A glaze defect displaying a fine network of cracks in the glaze.

Deflocculant. A base material, sodium silicate or soda ash, to be used to thin a clay slip.

Density. Weight per unit volume.

Dipping. A technique to glaze pottery by dipping it into the glaze solution.

Dry footing. An unglazed foot on a vessel. The removal with a sponge of excessive glaze from the foot of pottery.

Dunting. Cracking of the pottery by too rapid cooling.

Earthenware. The low-fire pottery fired under 2,000° F, usually made from red, or tan firing clays.

Engobe. Colored clays used for decoration on greenware.

Empirical formula. Glaze formulas expressed in molecular proportions.

Equivalent weight. The weight used in glaze calculations to produce one unit of a component of a particular chemical compound.

Faience. Earthenware covered with a lead-tin glaze. Originally made in Faenza, Italy.

Feldspar. The major source of insoluble alkali fluxes in glazes. Potash feldspar or Soda feldspar.

Filter press. A machine to remove excess water from slip to produce plastic clay.

Fire box. Combustion chamber of a fuel fired kiln.

Fire clay. A natural clay that will stand temperatures up to 3,000°.

Flint. Potters silica, usually finely ground quartz, provides the acids (glass-maker) in glazes.

Fluxes. The fusing agent in a clay-body, or, glaze that facilitates the melting.

Frit. Water-insoluble, partial glaze material which can be made into a complete glaze by the addition of kaolin or ball clay.

Glazes. A glassy surface coating fused to the clay-body during the final "glost" firing.

Greenware. Unfired, drying pottery.

Grog. Ground, fired fire clay usually added to clay bodies to reduce shrinkage.

Gum tragacanth. A natural binder added to glazes it facilitates their adherence to the clay during the handling before firing.

Incise. To cut or scratch a line into clay for decorative purposes.

Kaolin. Pure clay widely used in glazes and clay bodies. It fires white and is the chief ingredient in whiteware bodies.

Kiln. A furnace, a refractory chamber with burner attachments in which pottery is fired.

Leatherhard. The half-hard stage when clay is drying. It is still moist but no longer plastic.

Lusters. The irridescent effect achieved by a very thin layer of liquid metals applied to glazed pottery and refired.

Majolica glaze. A glossy, soft, opaque, low-fire glaze first used on the island of Majorca.

Mat glaze. A dull glaze without gloss, but pleasant to the eye and to the touch.

Maturing temperature. The temperature at which glaze ingredients enter into complete fusion, or when a clay body reaches optimum characteristics of density and strength with minimum warping and breakage.

Muffle kiln. A kiln with a refractory lining separating the flames from the wares.

Opacifier. A glaze ingredient causing an opaque appearance of the fired glaze through crystallization during firing. Tin oxide is the best known opacifier.

Oxide. A chemical compound of an element with oxygen.

Oxidizing fire. A firing during which the kiln chamber is allowed to retain a sufficient amount of oxygen.

Paste. European porcelain bodies.

Plaster of Paris. A gypsum cement which when combined with water hardens into a rocklike state.

Plasticity. The quality in clay of retaining any given shape.

Porcelain. A high-fire, hard, sometimes transluscent clay body which differs from other clay products because the bisque is always fired to a higher temperature than the glaze.

Potter's wheel. A revolving wheel on which vessels are formed from clay by hand.

Pug mill. A machine for mixing and pugging of clay, often combined with a de-airing chamber.

Pyrometer. An instrument for measuring of kiln temperatures.

Quartz. The rock source of silica, or potter's flint.

Raku. A soft, porous, heavily grogged earthenware with very low temperature glazes.

Raw Glazes. Frittless glazes. Glazes made directly from the ingredient compounds without the fritting of the materials.

Reduction firing. A firing with an atmosphere in the kiln chamber deficient of oxygen and rich in carbon particles. A smoky atmosphere.

Refractory. Heat resistant.

Semivitreous ware. Common white dinner ware also called semi porcelain.

Sgraffito. A decorating technique in which designs are "scratched" into the leatherhard clay sometimes through engobes to create two tone effects.

Short clay. Low on plasticity.

Silica. Ground quartz, the main ingredient in glazes. The Glass "making" factor in the glaze. SiO_2.

Slip. Sieved, liquid clay, usually used for casting in molds.

Slip decoration. Painting and trailing of colored slips on the unfired clay object.

Slurry. Unsieved, raw, liquid clay.

Stain. Ceramic color used in glazes and clay bodies.

Stilt. Mostly a three-legged refractory setter to elevate clay objects from the kiln floor during the glaze firing.

Stoneware. High-fire pottery made from a hard, dense body which is not transluscent like procelain.

Template. A tool, or guide shaped to fit special curves and forms.

Terra Cotta. A coarse, red firing clay body. Unglazed earthenware sculpture.

Throwing. The process to form pottery on the potter's wheel.

Turning. The process of turning or shaping pottery in a chuck or on a lathe.

Underglaze colors. Stains or colors applied directly to the bisque and made permanent by the glaze.

Viscosity. The non-running quality of a glaze during firing. Viscosity is influenced by the proportions of fluxes and alumina in a given glaze.

Wedging. The hand method for kneading clay.

Warping. The distortion of a pot during the firing because of faulty clay composition, or drafts in the kiln chamber.

Wax resist. A decorating method for pottery using the principle of resistance of water to fatty substances as wax.

Weathering. The breaking down of clay into small particles due to the influence of the elements.